Foreword

This Exam Preparation book is intended for those preparing for the Citrix XenApp 5.0 for Windows Server 2008 certification.

This book is **not** a replacement for completing the course. This is a study aid to assist those who have completed an accredited course and preparing for the exam.

Do not underestimate the value of your own notes and study aids. The more you have, the more prepared you will be.

While it is not possible to pre-empt every question and content that may be asked in the Citrix XenApp A05 exam, this book covers the main concepts covered within the Citrix XenApp discipline.

Due to licensing rights, we are unable to provide actual A05 exam. However, the study notes and sample exam questions in this book will allow you to more easily prepare for an A05 exam.

Ivanka Menken
Executive Director
The Art of Service

Notice of Liability

The information in this book is distributed on an “As Is” basis without warranty. While every precaution has been taken in the preparation of the book, neither the author nor the publisher shall have any liability to any person or entity with respect to any loss or damage caused or alleged to be caused directly or indirectly by the instructions contained in this book or by the products described in it.

Trademarks

Many of the designations used by manufacturers and sellers to distinguish their products are claimed as trademarks. Where those designations appear in this book, and the publisher was aware of a trademark claim, the designations appear as requested by the owner of the trademark. All other product names and services identified throughout this book are used in editorial fashion only and for the benefit of such companies with no intention of infringement of the trademark. No such use, or the use of any trade name, is intended to convey endorsement or other affiliation with this book.

Write a review to receive any *free* eBook from our Catalogue - $99 Value!

If you recently bought this book we would love to hear from you! Benefit from receiving a free eBook from our catalogue at http://www.emereo.org/ if you write a review on Amazon (or the online store where you purchased this book) about your last purchase!

How does it work?

To post a review on Amazon, just log in to your account and click on the Create your own review button (under Customer Reviews) of the relevant product page. You can find examples of product reviews in Amazon. If you purchased from another online store, simply follow their procedures.

What happens when I submit my review?

Once you have submitted your review, send us an email at review@emereo.org with the link to your review, and the eBook you would like as our thank you from http://www.emereo.org/. Pick any book you like from the catalogue, up to $99 RRP. You will receive an email with your eBook as download link. It is that simple!

Table of Contents

1. Citrix Certified Administrator

The Citrix Certified Administrator certification series is a number of certifications designed for IT associates spanning several Citrix solutions. Each certification is product based and consists of 3 designations:

- Citrix Certified Administrator
- Citrix Certified Administrator Platinum
- Citrix Certified Advanced Administrator

The topics of the administrative series are:

- Application Virtualization
- Desktop Virtualization
- Server Virtualization
- Application Networking

This study guide focuses on topics relevant to Application Virtualization and the core product, XenApp. The A05 exam is designed for persons in the following roles:

- Systems Administrators
- Technical Support staff
- Systems Integrators
- Citrix Consultants and Architects
- Sales Representatives
- Systems Engineers

Individuals taking the exam should already have an understanding of:

- Windows Server 2003 and 2008 configurations
- Microsoft Active Directory permissions and rights
- TCP protocol administration
- Firewall concepts
- Email administration and account creation
- Terminal Services
- Shared folders and files
- Basic database concepts

The exam covers:

- Citrix Architecture
- XenApp Licensing and Installing
- Web interface Configurations
- ICA Configurations
- Application Management
- XenApp policies
- Server and Server Farm Management
- Printing configuration
- XenApp Troubleshooting

2. Exam Specifics

A05 Exams are proctored by Pearson VUE. Scheduling and location of test sites can be obtained at www.vue.com. Tests are conducted at a testing center. Two valid forms of ID are required when arriving at the center. In addition, many Oracle University locations offer exams in addition to training.

Exams are delivered in a secure environment, proctored, and timed.

Specifics about the exam are:

- Exam Number : 1Y0-A05
- Time Limit: 105 minutes (English-speaking)
  135 minutes (Non-English speaking)
- # of Questions: 81
- Question Type: Multiple Choice
- Passing Score: 78%

If a candidate fails an exam on the first attempt, they must wait 24 hours before retaking the exam. Failure on any further attempts requires a 14 calendar day period before retaking the exam.

3. Windows Fundamentals

3.1 User Accounts

Several characteristics of user accounts should be understood:

- A unique Security Identifier (SID) is assigned to every user account.
- The Security Identifier is never reused.
- Because the SID never changes, an account can be renamed without losing any of the permissions assigned to it.
- User, computer, and group accounts are created and managed using the Active Directory Users and Computers MMC.
- The Local Users and Groups snap-in is used to create local users and groups.
- To import and export users and groups, csvde and ldifde are used.

3.1.1 Password Complexity

The complexity of passwords is determined by the domain account policies. When enabled, passwords must follow the minimum requirements:

- Must not contain all or part of the user's account name.
- Must be at least six characters in length.

- Must contain characters from three of four categories:
    - Uppercase characters
    - Lowercase characters
    - Numerals
    - Symbols

3.1.2 Managing User Profiles

User profiles are files where the settings for a user's work environment are stored. It is automatically created the first time a user logs on to a computer running any version of Windows. Any changes to the environment are saved when the user logs off and reloaded when the user logs on again.

The components of the user profile are:

- Application Data - program-specific data
- Cookies – user information and preferences
- Desktop – desktop items
- Favorites – shortcuts to favorite Internet locations
- Local Settings – application data, history, temporary files
- My Documents – user documents and subfolders
- My Recent Documents – shortcuts to most recently access documents and folders
- NetHood – shortcuts to My Network Places items
- PrintHood – shortcuts to printer folder items
- SendTo – shortcuts to document-handling utilities

- Start Menu – shortcuts to program items
- Templates – user template items

3.1.3 Profile Types

Several users can use the same computer running Windows because of the user profile facility. There are several profile types available:

- Roaming – for users who log to different computers on the network.
- Mandatory – for administrative enforcement of settings. Can be shared by two or more users.
- Local – created for every user at first logon.
- Temporary – for users who cannot load their profile.
- All Users – created for all users who log on to the computer.
- Default – created for users who log on for the first time.

3.1.4 Local Profiles

When a user logs on to a computer, a local profile is created and saved in the local Documents and Settings folder for that user. This is done whether the computer is connected to the network or not. Any changes to the profile are saved when the user logs off.

The contents of the “All users” files and folders are combined with the user's profile when the user logs on to the computer. The contents include the Start Menu and desktop items.

A profile can be turned into a template to create a default profile for a new user.

3.1.5 Roaming Profiles

The roaming profile is stored on a server. Each user account has a Profile tab in its properties sheet to identify a network location to use as a roaming profile.

When a user logs on to a network computer, the profile is copied locally to the computer. When the user logs off the network, any changes to the profile are copied back to the server.

3.1.6 Mandatory Profiles

A mandatory profile is a roaming profile that cannot be changed by the user. To create a mandatory profile, create a roaming profile and rename the Ntuser.dat file to Ntuser.man.

Like the roaming profile, a mandatory profile is stored on a server. When a user logs on to a network computer, the profile is copied locally to the computer. No changes are saved when the user logs off the server.

Any changes to the mandatory profile must be made by the Administrator.

3.2 Managing Groups

3.2.1 Domain Functionality Levels

There are four Domain Functionality Levels in Windows Server 2003:

- Windows 2000 mixed
- Windows 2000 native
- Windows Server 2003
- Windows Server 2003 interim

The default domain functionality level of a domain installed on a new Windows Server 2003 machine is Windows 2000 mixed which contain domain controllers on computers running Windows NT, Windows 2000, or Windows Server 2003. There is no enhanced group functionality at this level.

When all Windows NT domain controllers have been removed from the domain, the domain functionality level can be increased to Windows 2000 native or Windows Server 2003. The Windows 2000 native level allows improved group capabilities of Active Directory with the ability to "nest" groups and make available groups of Universal scope.

The Windows Server 2003 level is the most advanced level of domain functionality. Only domains with no Windows 2000 or Windows NT domain controllers can be raised to this level.

The fourth level of domain functionality is the Windows Server 2003 interim. Windows NT and Windows Server 2003 domain controllers can exist on this level at the expense of enhanced group functionality.

3.2.2 Group Types

There are two types of groups in Windows:

- Distribution – used for email distribution lists only and cannot be used to assign permissions for resource access.
- Security – used to assign permissions for resource access and for email distribution.

3.2.3 Group Scope

A group is classified using its scope. The scope determines what locations the members come from and the locations of the resources the group can be granted access. The group scopes are:

- Domain Local
- Global
- Universal

The scope of Domain Local will grant access to resources in the local domain and includes any account, Global groups, and Universal groups from any domain, or other Domain Local groups from the same domain as the group object.

A global group can be granted to any resource in the forest or any domain in another forest that trusts the local domain. The members are based on the domain functionality level used. For Windows 2000 mixed and Windows Server 2003 interim levels, only accounts from the same domain as the group object can be members. In the Windows 2000 native or Windows Server 2003 levels, accounts and other global groups from the same domain as the group object can be members.

3.2.4 Domain Groups

The Default Local Groups in Windows Server include:

- Administrators have unrestricted access to the computer, including the Domain Admins Global Group.
- Backup Operators are allowed to run Windows Backup and can override other rights when performing backups.
- Guests have restricted usage of the computer and limited to explicitly granted rights. The group can include the Domain Guests Global Groups.
- Power Users can share resources and create or modify local user accounts

- Users have limited use of the computer to include personal files and folders and explicitly granted rights. The group can include Domain User Global groups.

Windows Servers has some built-in special groups including:

- Anonymous Logon to not provide any default access rights and granted to user accounts that Windows XP cannot authenticate locally.
- Authenticated users are not given any default access rights and granted to users with valid local user accounts on the current computer.
- Creator Owners are an administrators group with designated full control over resources created or taken over by a member of the Administrators group.
- Dialup are for all users who have connected to the computer using a dial-up connection and have no specific rights.
- Everyone is for all users who access the computer and the default permission granted is Full Control. To deny any access this permission must be removed.
- Interactive has no specific rights and granted to users who have logged on locally to the computer.
- Network has no specific rights and granted to users who have established a connection to the computer's shared resource from a remote network computer.

3.2.5 Managing Group Membership

When rights are granted to domain users, use the AGDLP method:

- Place accounts in Global Groups.
- Place Global groups into Domain Local groups.
- Grant or deny permissions to the Domain Local group.

The Deny permission overrides all other permissions for groups that a specific user or group may be members of. Therefore, if a user belongs to two groups where one explicitly grants access to a resource and the other explicitly denies access to the same resource, the user will be unable to access the resource. They will see an access denied message.

3.2.6 Group Policy

The use of a Group Policy enables a standard collection of settings to be defined and applied to some or all the computers and/or users in the enterprise. A Group Policy provides centralized control of a variety of components of a Windows network related to security, application deployment and management, communications, and overall user experience.

A Group Policy is applied by creating an object that contains the settings that control the users' and computers' access to network and machine resources. The Group Policy Object (GPO) is created from templates stored on the workstation or server.

GPOs are linked to a container that holds Active Directory objects, such as users, groups, workstations, servers, and printers. The settings of the GPO are applied to the objects in the container which can be an Organization Unit (OU), a domain, or a site.

Using a Local Policy can apply GPOs with a single computer. Multiple GPOs can be applied to a single container, essentially merging the settings. If a conflict exists between different GPOs, the last setting applied is honored.

Group Policies work by manipulating Registry and security settings on a workstation or server. The Registry is not changed permanently, like system Policies used in Windows NT. After a Group Policy is removed, the Registry settings return to their default.

3.2.7 Group Policy Objects

Each GPO has two sections:

- User Configuration
- Computer Configuration

Some considerations about GPOs are:

- Some settings are available in both user and computer configurations. User settings will generally take precedence when conflicts occur.
- GPOs are stored in two parts: as part of the Group Policy Template (GPT) and as objects inside a container of the Active Directory called the GROUP Policy Container (GPC).
- GPTs contain settings related to software installation policies and deployments, scripts and security information for each GPO.
- GPTs are stored in the %SystemRoot%\SYSVOL\domain\Policies directory of every domain controlled and contain subfolders called Adm, USER, and MACHINE to separate data.
- The USER portion of the GPO is applied to keys in the HKEY_CURRENT_USER and the MACHINE portion is applied to keys in the HKEY_LOCAL_MACHINE.
- GPOS can be used to control servers and workstations installed with Windows 2000 or later.

3.2.8 GPO User Configurations

User settings are applied at user logon and during the periodic refresh cycle of the Group Policy. The settings are applied to a user on whatever computer the user logs on to.

The settings for users in a Group Policy apply to:

- Operating system behavior
- Desktop settings
- Security settings
- Application settings
- Application installation
- Folder redirection settings
- Logon and logoff scripts

3.2.9 GPO Computer Configurations

The settings for computers in a Group Policy apply to:

- Operating system behavior
- Desktop settings
- Security settings
- Application settings
- Application installation
- Folder redirection settings
- Computer startup and shutdown scripts

3.2.10 GPO Types

Two types of GPOs exist:

- Local
- Domain

Local GPOs apply to the computer first. If a conflict exists, the settings of the last GPO applied are honored. Group Policy in Windows works according to a hierarchy, called SDOU:

- Site
- Domain
- OU

The effects of Group Policy are cumulative.

There are two default GPOs in Windows Server:

- Default Domain Policy – linked to domains and controls the default account policies such as Password Policy and Account Lockout.
- Domain Controllers Policy – linked to Domain Controllers OU and contains settings for domain controllers only.

3.2.11 GPO Updates

Changes made to existing GPOs and new GPOs are applied during the refresh cycle with the following exceptions:

- Software installation and folder redirection settings are updated only at reboot and logon.
- Computer configuration changes will be refreshed every 16 hours despite being changed or not.
- Domain controllers refresh Group Policies every five minutes to prevent any delay to critical settings.

Changes can be implemented immediately using the gpupdate tool using the following command-line options:

- /Target:{Computer|User} specifies that only user of computers policy settings are refreshed.
- /Force reapplies all policy settings.
- /Wait:{value} sets the number of seconds to wait for policy processing to finish.
- /Logoff causes a logoff after settings are refreshed.
- /Boot causes a computer to restart after settings are refreshed.
- /Sync causes the next foreground policy to be done synchronously.

3.2.12 GPO Considerations

Active Directory objects lower in the hierarchy will inherit the settings from objects higher in the hierarchy. The Block Policy Inheritance option is set on a per-container basis and will block all policy inheritance.

The No Override option in a Group Policy prevents a child container from blocking the GPO inherited from the parent. This option can be set on a per-GPO basis.

Group Policy Filtering restricts the application of a GPO by applying permissions on the GPO that can be used by specified users, computers, or groups. For a Group Policy to be applied to an object, at least Read permissions for the GPO must be in place.

3.3 Shared Files and Folders

3.3.1 Share Permissions

Share permissions apply when a file or folder is accessed over a network through a shared folder. A shared folder is granted Read access to the Everyone group by default. Only Administrators, Server Operators, and Power users group are permitted to share folders.

The only permissions allowed for a shared folder are:

- Read
- Change
- Full Control

When accessing the contents of a shared folder on a NTFS volume, the effective permission of the object is the combined shared and NTFS permissions of the object. The effective permission will always be the most restrictive.

3.3.2 Encrypting File System (EFS)

Encrypting File System (EFS) allows a user to selectively encrypt files and folders as desired. After a file is encrypted, all file operations continue transparently for the user who performed the encryption. Unauthorized users will not be able to access the files.

Though EFS encryption is similar to NTFS compression, they are mutually exclusive to each other, preventing a file or folder from being compressed and encrypted at the same time.

Some other considerations include:

- A Certificate Authority (CA) is required to deploy EFS.
- Only files and folders on NTFS volumes can be encrypted.
- If a folder is encrypted, all files and folders in that folder are encrypted automatically.

- Encrypted files will be unencrypted when moved or copied to a non-NTFS volume.
- Encrypted files moved or copied to an unencrypted folder on an NTFS volume will not be unencrypted.
- A recovery agent is any authorized individual who is able to decrypt data when the original certificate is unavailable.
- A recovery agent is any user assigned to that role.

Encrypted files can be shared with the following considerations:

- When a user is given permission to a file, the user can grant others permission to use the file.
- Encrypted files can be shared. Encrypted folders cannot be shared, except when an NTFS file share.
- Any user granted access must have an EFS certificate which resides in Active Directory, the user's roaming profile, or user's profile on the server where the shared file is located.

3.3.3 File System Permissions

Permissions define the type of access granted to a user or group for an object (file, folder, or share). Permissions are assigned to local users or groups, or for servers who are members of a domain, any user or group that is trusted by the domain.

At a server or workstation console, the NTFS file and folder access permissions are the only concerns of the administrator. When accessing files across the network through a shared folder, file and share permissions apply.

3.3.4 NTFS Permissions

The following permissions apply to files, folders, and subfolders:

- Read – the contents of the file or folder and its attributes can be read, including ownership and assigned permissions.
- Read and Execute – In addition to all Read permission capabilities, the ability to run applications applies.
- Write – In addition to all Read permission capabilities, the ability to overwrite the file or folder and change its attributes applies.
- Modify – In addition to all Read and Execute and Write permission capabilities, the ability to modify or delete the file or folder applies.
- Full Control. In addition to all Modify permission capabilities, the ownership of the file or folder can be taken over and the permission configuration of the file or folder changed.

3.3.5 File or Folder Ownership

A creator or owner of a file of folder will automatically have Full Control permission for the object. Special permissions can be added to provide even granular access to an object. Special permissions are typically a subset of the basic NTFS permissions. Owners always have the right to modify permissions.

3.3.6 Inherited Rights

Inherited rights are the permissions that apply to a file or folder based on their placement in the file hierarchy. There are some rules to be aware of:

- Folder permissions are inherited by subfolders unless the 'This Folder Only' option is selected when applying the permissions.
- A user's actual permissions are the result of the collective allowed rights flowing down from upper-level folders plus any explicitly assigned permission at that level.
- Denied rights override allowed rights
- Explicit permissions always override inherited permissions

When file and folder permissions are assigned, the permissions are automatically applied to the files and folders underneath them in the hierarchy, except when the rules above apply.

3.3.7 Permissions when Copying or Moving

When a file or folder is copied or moved, its permissions may be changed under the following rules:

- The original permissions are retained when a file or folder is moved to another location on the same NTFS volume.
- The permissions of the new parent folder are inherited when a file or folder is copied to another location on the same NTFS volume.
- The permissions of the new parent folder are inherited when a file or folder is moved to a different NTFS volume.
- The permissions of the new parent folder are inherited when a file or folder is copied to a different NTFS volume.

3.4 Terminal Services

Windows Terminal Services distribute the Windows 32-bit desktop to clients unable to run it. Though the application appears locally for the user, the processing required is performed at the server. At the client, the only processing done displays the user interface and accepting input for the keyboard or mouse.

3.4.1 Components of Terminal Services

Terminal Services is comprised of three major components:

- Multiuser Server Core – a modified version of the Windows Server kernel that allows support of multiple concurrent users and share resources.
- Client Software – called the Remove Desktop Connection (RDC) client software, it provides the user interface. It is installed on a PC, a Windows terminal, or handheld device and has the look and feel of the standard Windows interface.
- Remote Desktop Protocol (RDP) – provides the required communication between server and client software. It will only run on TCP/IP.

3.4.2 Modes of Terminal Services

The modes of Terminal Services are:

- Remote Desktop for Administration (previously known as Remote Administration mode).
- Application Server.

Remote Desktop for Administration mode provides remote server management and is automatically installed in Windows Server. Incoming connections are disabled by default. Two concurrent sessions are allowed along with a console session to the Windows server.

Application Server mode requests a Windows Server Terminal Services user or device Client Access License (TS CAL) at each remote connection. The Client Access License is separate from the normal Windows Client Access licenses (CALs) and must be installed and managed using a Terminal Services licensing server. The license must be installed within 90 days to allow the client to access the server.

To install applications on a Terminal Services server in Application Server mode, the Install mode must be accessed. This can be done by installing programs using the Add/Remove Programs applet or using the Change User command.

When connecting through a RDC client, the resources that can be mapped between server and client are:

- Client drives
- Client printers
- Clipboard
- Printers
- Serial ports
- Sound

3.4.3 Licensing Servers

The two types of Terminal Services licensing servers built into Windows Server are:

- Enterprise License server – used when Terminal Services are located in several domains and is the default licensing server.
- Domain License server – used if licensing is segregated by domain or a Windows NT 4.0 domain or a workgroup is supported.

3.5 Windows Printing

3.5.1 Print Queue Definitions

Some key terms related to print queues are:

- Print job – the sequence of data and print device commands sent to a print device.
- Spooler – the service managing the documents that are waiting to be printed.
- Spool file – the file which stores the print data while waiting to be printed.
- Print queue – the list of print jobs currently in the spooler.
- Print server – a computer where print drivers are installed and shared.

- Printer driver – the software enabling the operating system to communicate to the printing device.
- Print device – the physical printer connected to the computer.
- Local printer – any print device that is directly attached to and controlled by the print server.
- Network printer – any print device directly attached to the network.

3.5.2 Printer Pooling

Printer pooling is a form of load balancing where two or more print devices are represented by a single virtual printer. When users send a print job to the printer, the print server queues the print job in the order submitted. For successful print pooling:

- The printers must use the same print driver.
- The printers must be connected to the same print server.
- The printers should be located in close proximity to each other.

Several logical printers can be attached to a single physical printer. Each logical printer must use the same print driver but can have slightly different configurations and be assigned to different people.

3.5.3 Roles and Priorities

Different users can be assigned to different logical printers with different priorities. Priorities can be set from 1 to 00 and define the default importance of the print jobs in the queue. The job with the highest priority will be printed first.

Roles are used to classify different sets of users. Roles can be applied to an individual or group. Roles can be configured to allow the abilities to print, manage document, or manage printers. Some pre-defined group-specific roles include:

- Administrators – full access
- Creator Owner – manage documents only
- Everyone – print only
- Power users – full access
- Print Operators – full access
- Server Operators – full access

3.5.4 Printer Properties

The advanced properties that can be configured are:

- Always available and Available from – specifies the hours of the day the printer is available.
- Priority – assigns a numerical priority to the printer.

- Spool print documents so program finishes printing faster – enables spooling of documents, either printing immediately or after last page is spooled.
- Print directly to the printer – no spooling performed.
- Hold mismatched documents – documents not matching the available form are held.
- Print spooled documents first – Prints documents in order they finish spooling, not start spooling.
- Keep printed documents – printed jobs are retained in the spooler.
- Enable advanced printing features – provides options like page order and pages per sheet.
- Printing Defaults command button – default orientation and order of pages can be selected.
- Print Processor command button – the available print processes can be specified.
- Separator Page command button – allows a separator page file to be specified.

3.5.5 Print Spooler

Print spoolers are a service which is part of the operating system. The service manages print queues for all local or network printers managed by the server.

The spool file is located at %systemroot%\system32\Spool\Printers.

A significant impact on network and print server loads can be generated because of large print jobs. On a Windows Server 2003 print server, the print spooler files can be relocated to a dedicated hard disk is loads are high.

3.5.6 Print Management Console

Introduced with Windows Server 2003 R2, the Print Management Console (PMC) is an updated Microsoft Management Console (MMC) snap-in. The snap-in can be used to view and manage printers and print servers in the organization. Print Management can be used from any computer running Windows Server 2003 R2 or later. Any network printer running Windows 2000 Server, Windows Server 2003 or Windows Server 2003 R2 can be managed through Print Management.

The Print Management Console is not installed by default and must be manually installed after the initial installation of Windows Server.

Included with the PMC is the Printer Filters feature which can group printers based on various criteria to be found and managed easily. The preconfigured printer filters include:

- All Printers – contains all printers in the organization.
- Printers Not Ready – shows any printer in a not ready condition because of an error, being paused, out of paper, or other reason.

- Printers with Jobs – shows all printers with print jobs currently in their print queues.

3.6 TCP/IP Model

The TCP/IP model consists of four layers with several sublayers. TCP/IP layers correlate roughly to OSI reference model and include the layers:

- Application Layer
- Transport Layer
- Internetwork Layer
- Network Interface Layer

The model defines a collection of protocols to enable communications across the network. Each protocol is defined in detail in Requests for Comments (RFC) documents. By implementing RFCs, a computer implements standard networking protocols defined by TCP/IP that enable communication with other computers implementing TCP/IP.

3.6.1 TCP/IP Application Layer

The TCP/IP Application layer correlates to OSI Application, Presentation, and Session layers and provides the interface between the network and the application. The layer enables communication services to applications and is responsible for the controlling communications and presentation of data. The HTTP, PO3, and

SMTP protocols are contained in this layer.

3.6.2 TCP/IP Transport Layer

The TCP/IP Transport layer correlates to the OSI Transport layer. It provides functionality in flow control, error recovery, and choice of protocols. Flow control is done by sending data at a rate that is allowed by the network or protocol selection to prevent congestion. Multiplexing of incoming data is performed if a packet arrives out of order, a packet is reordered. The transport layer uses TCP and UCP protocols.

3.6.3 TCP/IP Internetwork Layer

The TCP/IP Internetwork layer correlates to the OSI Network Layer, to define logical addressing, end-to-end delivery of packets, routing architecture, and the process for fragmenting a packet. The IP and ICMP protocols are found on this layer.

3.6.4 TCP/IP Network Interface Layer

The TCP/IP Network Interface Layer correlates to the OSI Data Link and Physical Layers and focuses on the physical characteristics of the transmission medium. The layer is concerned with transmitting data across a link or medium, defining delivery across an individual link and physical layer specifications. The Ethernet and Frame Relay protocols are in this layer.

3.7 Network Protocols

3.7.1 Transmission Control Protocol (TCP)

The Transmission Control Protocol is a core component of the Internet Protocol Suite, TCP/IP. TCP focuses on the reliable, ordered delivery of bytes from one computer to another program on another computer. E-mail and file transfer are common applications of TCP because of its ability to control segment size, flow control, rate of data exchange, and network congestion.

As mentioned, TCP is part of the larger TCP/IP suite. The Internet Protocol (IP) is designed to exchange pieces of information in the form of packets, which are sequences of bytes combined with a header and body. The header describes the destination of the packet and is used to forward the packet through the network. The body contains the data being transmitted.

When a large amount of data must be sent across the network, the data can be broken up into several pieces and requests that can be handled by IP. TCP can be used to create a single request and handle all the IP details to transmit the data. This process prevents the problems of IP packets becoming lost or delivered out of order. TCP will detect when these problems happen, request retransmission of lost packets, reorder packets, and minimizes network congestion.

3.7.2 File Transfer Protocol (FTP)

File Transfer Protocol is a network protocol for exchanging and manipulating files over a TCP/IP based network. FTP is found within client-server architectures and will utilize separate control and data connections between the application on the client and server sides of the connection.

The use of FTP is driven by the desire to:

- Promote sharing of files
- Encourage use of remote computing
- Shield users from variations in file storage systems
- Transfer data reliably and efficiently

FTP works in two different transport modes to form a control stream that defines the parameters for sending data. In active mode, the FTP client opens a dynamic port to send the FTP server the dynamic port number and waits for a connection. When the data connection is initiated by the server, the client will bind the source port to port 20 on the FTP server. In passive mode, the FTP server will open a dynamic port and send the FTP client the server's IP address to connect to the port which the server is listening. When the client makes the connection, it binds the source port to the dynamic port. Extended passive mode works just like passive mode, but only the port number is transmitted.

While data is being transferred through a data stream, the control stream sits idle which can cause problems with timing out with large data transfers across the firewall.

3.7.3 Trivial File Transfer Protocol (TFTP)

The Trivial File Transfer Protocol is a simpler version of FTP that can be implemented with very little memory. It is an excellent tool for transmitting small amounts of data between network hosts, specifically thin clients and IP phones. TFTP is also used to load basic kernel that will later perform the action installation of a program.

TFTP utilizes UDP and supplies its own transport and session support. The UDP port 69 is its transport protocol. Its primary purpose is to read files from remote servers and write files to remote servers. Unfortunately, its lack of security makes it vulnerable in open Internet sessions and therefore typically restricted to use in private, local networks. Unlike its FTP counterpart, TFTP cannot list directory contents and has no mechanisms for authentication or encryption.

3.7.4 User Datagram Protocol (UDP)

User Datagram Protocol is part of the Internet Protocol Suite. With UDP, computer applications will send messages in the form of datagrams to other hosts on an IP network. Special transmission channels or data paths are not required to send communication.

Also called the Universal Datagram Protocol, UDP uses a simple transmission model without the handshakes required for guaranteeing reliability, ordering, or data integrity. Error checking is assumed to be performed at the application level and ignored by UDP. UDP is popular with time-sensitive data transmissions that can be delayed with error checking processes or to answer small queries from large numbers of clients that exist in packet broadcasting or multicasting. Several common network applications use UDP, such as DNS, IPTV, VoIP, TFTP and online games.

Datagram sockets are used to establish host-to-host communications by UDP applications. These sockets bind the application to service ports that act as endpoints for the data transmission. The packet of the UDP is structured with a header and body, or payload. Application multiplexing and integrity verification of the entire packet is provided, but reliability in the transmission is provided by the application. The UDP header consists of the source port, destination port, length, and checksum.

3.7.5 Dynamic Host Configuration Protocol (DHCP)

The Dynamic Host Configuration Protocol focuses on obtaining configuration information for device operation within an IP network. Used by network applications, DHCP reduces the administration workload and allows devices to be added to the network with little or no manual intervention.

Network parameters assignments to network devices can be automated through one or more DHCP servers. Clients configured for DHCP will send a broadcast query when connecting to the network requesting necessary information from a DHCP server. These servers manage pools of IP addresses and information about configuration parameters used by clients about default gateways, domain names, DNS servers, and other network specific information. The server will receive the broadcasted request from the client and assign an IP address, a lease defining the time length for the IP address and other IP configuration parameters, including the gateway and subnet mask. Allocation of IP addresses is done using one of three methods:

- Dynamic allocation – a range of IP addresses is assigned to DHCP and each client computer on the network is configured to request an IP address.
- Automatic allocation – a free IP address is permanently assigned to a request client by the DHCP server from a range defined by the administrator. The DHCP server maintains a table of past IP address assignments to

ensure that the same IP address be assigned to the same client.

- Static Allocation – IP addresses are allocated by the DHCP server based on a table with pairs of MAC addresses and IP addresses which are manually completed. Only clients with a MAC address listed in the table can request and be allocated an IP address.

3.7.6 Domain Name System (DNS)

The Domain Name System is a hierarchical naming system for computers, services and other resources connected to a network, namely the Internet of private network. The protocol is used to translate domain names to numerical identifiers (IP addresses) associated with networking equipment. This allows devices connected to the network to be located and addressed.

A domain name space is constructed like a tree of domain names. The tree is divided into zones starting with the root zone. Each DNS zone is a collection of connected nodes served by an authoritative nameserver. Responsibility over any zone can be divided and delegated into smaller zones, or domains.

Domain names are constructed in two or more parts. The rightmost label is the top-level domains, typically represented by a three character universally recognized label that identifies the type of domain devices reside. The most common labels are:

- .gov US Government entities
- .edu Post Secondary Educational organizations
- .com Commercial organizations
- .mil US Military
- .org Generic label (Miscellaneous)
- .net Network Infrastructures

The top level domains can be further represented by country specific codes utilizing the two character domains established by ISO 3166.

Domain names also include subdomains and hostnames that are associated to specific IP addresses.

3.7.7 Hypertext Transfer Protocol (HTTP)

Hypertext Transfer Protocol is an application-level protocol used to retrieve inter-linked resources allowing distribution and collaboration. HTTP uses a request and response system to operate. The client is an application or computer used by a user which requests information from a website hosted by a server. The server stores and creates resources which are accessible by HTTP. The protocol runs on top of other protocols, such as TCP. Resources are identified using Uniform Resource Identifiers (URIs) and Uniform Resource Locators (URLs).

When an HTTP client initiates a request with a Web server, it establishes a TCP connection through a port, usually port 80. A series of network request and response transactions are performed. The protocol defines eight methods that can be performed on a resource, including:

- HEAD – asks for an identical response to a Get response without a response body.
- GET – requests a representation of the resource.
- POST – submits data to be processed to the resource.
- PUT – uploads a representation of the resource.
- DELETE – deletes the resource.
- TRACE – allows changes from intermediate servers to be seen by echoing back the received request.
- OPTIONS – informs of the HTTP methods supported by the server for the specific URL and allows a functionality check of the web server.
- CONNECT – converts the request connection to a transparent TCP/IP tunnel.

3.7.8 Hypertext Transfer Protocol Secure (HTTPS)

Hypertext Transfer Protocol Secure is a combination of HTTP and the SSL/TLS protocol to enable encryption and secure identification of the server. Used extensively for payment transactions over the Web and other sensitive transactions, HTTPS is based on major certificate authorities installed in browser software. A HTTPS connection is considered secure and trusted if and only if:

- The user trusts the certificate authority to vouch for legitimate websites.

- The website can provide a valid certificate signed by a trusted authority.
- The certificate correctly identifies the website.
- The intervening hops between client and website are trustworthy.

3.7.9 Transport Layer Security (TLS)

Transport Layer Security is a cryptographic protocol which provides security for communications over the network by encrypting segments of the connection at the Transport layer. TLS is based on the Secure Sockets Layer (SSL) and is used in applications for web browsing, electronic mail, Internet faxing, instant messaging, and VoIP.

TLS is designed to prevent eavesdropping, tampering, and message forgery of Internet communications by providing endpoint authentication and communications confidentiality. TLS supports unilateral and bilateral authentication and involves three basic phases:

- Peer negotiation
- Key exchange and authentication
- Symmetric cipher encryption and message authentication

Different encryption algorithms can be used but must be agreed upon by both endpoints within a communication session.

TLS is used in conjunction with HTTP, FTP, and SMTP, running on top of them. It can be used with TCP or UDP. It is also used to create a Virtual Private Network by tunneling an entire network stack. SIP uses TLS to protect its application signaling.

3.7.10 Session Initiation Protocol (SIP)

Session Initiation Protocol is a signaling protocol used to control multimedia communication session over IP, such as voice and video calls. SIP will enable the creation, modification, and termination of two-party or multiparty sessions comprises of one or more media streams.

SIP utilizes several design elements to HTTP and STMP. It is a TCP/IP based application layer protocol that can run on top of TCP or UDP. Though SIP can work with several other protocols, it is only involved in the signaling portion of a communication session and used to construct and deconstruct voice or video calls. SIP applications utilize another application protocol, Real-Time Transport Protocol (RTP), to carry voice and video stream data. It supports the call processing functions and features found in public switched telephone network (PSTN) and operates similar to familiar telephone operation.

3.7.11 Real-Time Transport Protocol (RTP)

The Real-Time Transport Protocol defines the standardized packet format for delivering audio and video over the Internet. It is used in communication and entertainment systems involved with streaming media, such as telephony, video conferencing applications. RTP is designed to provide end-to-end, real-time, transfer of multimedia data.

The RTP specification describes two sub-protocols:

- Data Transfer Protocol – deals with the transfer of real-time multimedia data and enables timestamps, sequence numbers, and payload format.
- Real Time Control Protocol (RTCP) – specifies QoS feedback and synchronization between media streams.

For each multimedia stream, an RTP session is established consisting of an IP address with ports for both RTP and RTCP.

3.7.12 Simple Mail Transport Protocol (SMTP)

Simple Mail Transport Protocol is an Internet standard for electronic mail. Electronic mail servers and mail transfer units use SMTP to send and receive mail messages, but client mail applications use SMTP for sending messages to a mail server. To receive messages, client applications use POP or IMAP.

SMTP defines the transport of the message, not the content of the message. Using SMTP, e-mail is submitted from a message user agent (MUA), or the client's email application, to a mail server agent (MSA). The MSA will deliver the mail to a message transfer agent (MTA) which typically resides on the same mail server. SMTP uses port 587 to submit to MSAs and port 25 to transfer to MTAs. The MTA will search the DNS for destination mail exchanger records and relay the mail to the server. Once accepted the MTA will deliver the incoming message using a mail delivery agent (MDA) to the server designated for local mail delivery. The MDA will either store the mail or forward it over a network. An authenticated MUA is used to retrieve mail from the local mail server using POP or IMAP.

3.7.13 Post Office Protocol (POP3)

Post Office Protocol is an application-layer Internet standard to retrieve e-mail from a remote server over a TCP/IP connection. Several versions have been developed and POP3 is the current standard. The use of POP is typically associated with e-mail clients connecting to mail servers, retrieving all messages, storing those messages on the user's computer as new messages, deleting the messages from the server, and disconnecting from the mail server. Some clients have the option to continue storing messages on the server and synchronizing with the client using the POP3 Unique Identification Listing (UIDL) command.

3.7.14 Internet Message Access Protocol (IMAP)

The Internet Message Access Protocol (IMAP) is another application-layer message retrieval protocol. Unlike POP, IMAP supports both on-line and off-line modes of operations. Messages are generally left on the server until they are explicitly deleted. This allows multiple clients to access the same mailbox.

Most e-mail applications will support either POP or IMAP; however few Internet Service Providers (ISPs) support IMAP.

3.7.15 Telnet

Telnet is used to facilitate bidirectional interactive communications. Access to a command-line interface is provided. This interface is located on a remote host through a virtual terminal connection. Telnet works on TCP.

A connection to TCP port 23 is established by the protocol to a listening Telnet server application. The protocol does not encrypt any data and offers no authentication. These weaknesses have been the primary reasons for the decline in using Telnet; however, it is still used in diagnosing problems without using specialized client software. It can be used to debug network services for SMTP, IRC, HTTP, FTP, and POP.

3.7.16 Secure Shell (SSH)

A more secure protocol with the same functionality of Telnet, Secure Shell allows data to be exchanged using a secure channel between two networked devices. SSH is primarily used on Linux and Unix systems to access shell accounts. Public-key cryptography is used to authenticate remote systems and the user, if needed. Often used to log into remote systems and execute commands, SSH will support tunneling, forwarding TCP ports and X11 connections.

SSH-2 has three well-separated layers:

- Transport layer – handles initial key exchange and server authentication and establishes encryption, compression, and integrity verification.
- User Authentication layer -handles client authentication and several methods for authentication including password, public key, and keyboard-interactive.
- Connection layer – defines channels, channel requests, and global requests using SSH services.

3.7.17 Simple Network Management Protocol (SNMP)

Simple Network Management Protocol is a UDP-based network protocol used to monitor network-attached devices for conditions requiring attention of the network administrator. It is a component of the IP Suite and contains a set of standards for network management consistent with the application layer protocol, a database schema, and a set of data objects.

When using SNMP, one or more administrative computers can monitor or manage a group of hosts on the computer network. These managing systems are referred to as "Masters." The systems that are being managed are referred to as "Slaves" and will execute an agent that reports information through SNMP to the Masters.

The management data reported by the SNMP agents are viewed as variables and consist of such measures as free memory, system name, and number of running processes. These variables are organized in hierarchies that are described by Management Information Bases (MIBs).

3.7.18 Network Time Protocol (NTP)

Network Time Protocol is used to synchronize the clocks of computer systems over packet-switched, variable-latency data networks. Using UDP port 123, NTP is one of the oldest Internet protocol. It uses a hierarchical, layered system of clock sources. Each level of the hierarchy is referred to as a stratum and assigned a layer number. Each stratum will define its distance from the reference clock and will prevent cyclical dependencies. The different levels are:

- Stratum 0 – consists of atomic clocks, GPS clocks, or radio clocks that are directly connected to the local computer and not the network.

- Stratum 1 – computers attached to Stratum 0 devices which typically act as servers for timing requests from other levels. Often called time servers.
- Stratum 2 – consists of computers which send NTP requests to Stratum 1 servers.
- Stratum 3 – consists of computers which send NTP requests to Stratum 2 computers.

3.7.19 Internet Control Message Protocol (ICMP)

The Internet Control Message Protocol is used by operating systems on networked systems to send error messages. IP is used to perform the tasks of ICMP making the protocol an integral part of the IP. ICMP messages are a result of errors in IP datagrams and constructed at the Internet layer. The message usually uses the IP datagram with the ICMP response. IP will encapsulate the message with a new IP header and transmit back to the original sending host. The traceroute command and ping utility uses ICMP messaging to function.

3.7.20 Internet Group Management Protocol (IGMP)

The Internet Group Management Protocol is used by IP hosts and adjacent routers to establish memberships to multicast groups. As a communication protocol, it is used by client computers to connect to a local multicast router. Protocol Independent Multicast (PIM) is used to direct multicast traffic from the server to the clients.

3.7.21 Address Resolution Protocol (ARP)

The Address Resolution Protocol aids in determining a host's link layer or hardware address when only its IP address or Network Layer address is known. This is important for local area networking or routing internetworking traffic based on IP addresses when the next hop must be determined. Used in IPv4 networks (IPv6 uses the Neighbor Discovery Protocol (NDP), ARP is a request and response protocol that operates only across the local link that a host is connected to.

3.8 Networking

3.8.1 Network Traffic

Five areas are explored to characterize network traffic:

- Broadcast behavior
- Frame size
- Windowing
- Flow control
- Error-recovery mechanisms

Three types of broadcasts and multicasts include:

- From desktop protocols, such as AppleTalk, IP, IPX, and NetBIOS.
- From servers to advertise services.
- From routing protocols such as RIP.

Broadcasts and multicasts affect the CPU of network devices which have to process all the traffic, even if it's unnecessary.

With network design, the traffic can be separated to maximize bandwidth. Machines that generate more traffic should be limited per segment. Below are guidelines for the maximum number of workstations for each segment based on protocol:

- 500 workstations for IP segments.
- 300 workstations for IPX segments.
- 200 workstations for AppleTalk segments.
- 200 workstations for NetBIOS segments.
- 200 workstations for Mixed protocol segments.

Routers and other similar devices process frames by fragmenting and reassembling them when they are at a certain size.

Manipulating the frame size can improve network performance by making it the largest possible maximum transmission unit (MTU). Not all protocols will support MTU configuration so some caution is required to avoid too large a MTU.

Windowing and flow control are error-control methods used by network-layer protocols. A couple of approaches are used: the ping-pong approach generates a response for each requests using bandwidth and the burst-mode approach sends as much data as can be handled by the receiver.

Transmission Control Protocol (TCP) applications, such as FTP, Telnet, SMTP, and HTTP, use windowing and flow control. User Datagram Protocol (UDP), which is a layer 4 transport layer protocol, does not. UDP applications consist of SNMP, DNS, TFTP, RPC, and DHCP.

To ensure successful transmission of packets, a method called error recovery is used. Error recovery is used by connection-oriented protocol, but not some transport layer protocols. A protocol analyzer can be used to identify protocols effectively using error recovery.

3.8.2 Proxy Server

Proxy servers are used in networking environments to act as an intermediary between clients seeking resources and other servers. When a client connects to the proxy server, it requests a service or other resources which is available from a different server. The proxy server serves four purposes:

- To allow servers behind it to remain anonymous.
- To provides caching services to allow faster access to resources.

- To censor network services and content.
- To forge transmitted content before delivery.

If a proxy server passes requests and responses unmodified it is considered a tunneling proxy or gateway. Proxy servers can perform one or more additional functions:

- Caching Proxy – speeds up service requests by retrieving content saved from previous requests.
- Web Proxy – focuses on WWW traffic in order to cache.
- Content-filtering Web Proxy – provides administrative control over content.
- Hostile Proxy – eavesdrops on dataflow between client machines and the web.
- Intercepting Proxy – a proxy server with functions of a gateway or router.
- Forced Proxy – filters all traffic and forces the user to configure a proxy.
- Suffix Proxy – allows access to web content by appending the name of the process server to the URL.
- Reverse Proxy – Provides encryption/SSL acceleration, load balancing, compression, and traffic control to several web servers receiving Internet traffic.
- Tunneling Proxy – used to move through implemented blocking policies.

3.8.3 Peer-To-Peer Networks

Peer-to-Peer networks have no hierarchy of computers. Each computer on the network can act as a server or a client. Each user is responsible for the security and sharing functions of their individual computers. The networks are limited to 15-20 computers. The most popular operating systems supporting P2P networks are:

- Microsoft Windows for Workgroups
- Microsoft Windows 2000
- Novell's Netware
- UNIX
- Linux

3.8.4 Server/Client Networks

Server/Client networks consist of one or more dedicated computers used as servers. The servers manage the access to all shared files and peripherals. Network Operating Systems (NOS) manages security and provides access administration to resources. Clients on the network use the resources available by the servers. Common operating systems supporting Server/Client networks are:

- Microsoft Windows NT Server 4
- Microsoft Windows 2000
- Novell's Netware

3.8.5 Virtual Private Network (VPN)

When two hosts want to communicate securely over an untrusted network, they can use an encrypted tunnel called a Virtual Private Network (VPN). This is a popular solution for remote users, but also to mask the IP address of individual computers usually to browse the Web anonymously. The links between nodes are formed over logical connections or virtual circuits between hosts of the larger network.

VPNs utilize a suite of protocols, called IP Security (IPSec), to communication securely using IP. IPSec provides mechanisms for authentication and encryption. Standard IPSec will only authenticate hosts with each other. Organizations must deploy a nonstandard proprietary IPSec implementation, or use L2TP (Layer 2 Tunneling Protocol) to encapsulate IPSec packets within.

The authentication header (AH) plays an important part in ensuring that the packet has not been tampered. The AH ensures the integrity of the packet, not the confidentiality.

Confidentiality is aided by the encapsulated security payload (ESP) which encrypts IP packets and ensures integrity. Both services are optional, though one must be used. ESP contains for sections:

- ESP header – contains information about security association and sequence number.
- ESP payload – the encrypted part of the packet.
- ESP trailer – padding of required by encryption algorithm.

- Authentication – a filed containing the integrity check value (hash).

Security associations (SA) define the mechanisms used by an endpoint to communicate. They cover one-way transmissions only. To communicate in the opposite direction, a second SA must be used.

To communicate with IPSec, endpoints use either transport or tunnel mode. Transport mode protects the IP payload only, while tunnel mode protects both the payload and IP header. Tunnel mode is typically found in transmissions between networks.

3.8.6 Virtual LANs

Virtual LANs are a flat network topology creating a single broadcast domain and act as a fully Layer 2 switched network. The more hosts in the network, the more broadcast domains. Redundancies for load balancing and fault tolerance are not available.

Virtual LANs (VLANs) allow switched network to be subdivided into logical groupings. Each subdivided network becomes a single broadcast domain. All devices connected to a VLAN receive broadcasts from other devices on the VLAN and broadcasts from other VLANs are not received.

Members of the VLAN can be connected anywhere in the network as long as connectivity is provided. Layer 2 switches have VLAN mappings and will provide logical connectivity.

End-users must be able to gain membership to a VLAN and can do so through two methods: static VLANs and dynamic VLANs.

Static VLANs offer port-based membership. Switch ports are assigned to specific VLANs. End devices will automatically assume VLAN connectivity when a port is connected. No handshaking or unique VLAN membership protocol needed. Membership is handled by hardware with application specific integrated circuits (ASICs) in the switch. Static VLANs provide good performance because all port mappings are done at the hardware level.

Dynamic VLANs provide membership based on MAC address. This allows the greatest flexibility and mobility, but requires more administrative overhead. When connected, a device must query a database to establish membership. A network administrator will assign a MAC address to a VLAN in the VLAN Membership Policy Server (VPS) database.

The number of VLANs implemented are influenced by:

- Traffic patterns
- Application types
- Common workgroup segmentation
- Network management requirements
- Relationship between VLANs and IP addressing schemes

VLANs can be scaled in the switch block using: end-to-end VLANs and local VLANs. End-to-end VLANs span the entire switch fabric and is also know as a campus-wide VLAN. It supports maximum flexibility and mobility of end devices. Users connecting to the networks are assigned regardless of physical location.

Local VLANs enables access to central resources outside their VLANs. Typically, more traffic goes through the network core. It is designed to contain user communities by geography, regardless of traffic leaving the VLAN. The size of the VLAN ranges from a single switch to entire buildings.

3.9 Firewall Concepts

3.9.1 Packet Filtering

Packet filtering is implemented on routers and layer 3 devices to identify if specific packets will be blacked or forwarded at each interface. The decisions for filtering the packets are based on information rules contained in the Access Control List (ACL). Standard access lists will not filter on transport layer information. To filter using a protocol or related parameter, extended ACLs are used. UDP filtering is based on port numbers. TCP filtering can be done using:

- Established connections
- Port numbers or number ranges
- Type of service

3.9.2 IP Access Control List

Access Control Entries (ACEs) are processed by routers sequentially. Packets are either permitted or denied based on the first ACE matched by the packet in the Access Control List. For an individual ACE, all configured values must match before it can be considered to be a match.

To create an individual ACE, IP ACL permit and deny commands are used. Port is important for determining the appropriate command. The Port Number field can only be matched when the protocol type in an extended IP ACL. ACE is TCP or UDP. The source port matching parameter must occur right after the source IP address, and the destination port matching parameter must occur right after the destination IP address. Some of the keywords for IP ACE port matching are:

- gt – greater than
- lt – less than
- eq – equal to
- ne – not equal to
- range x-y – inclusive range of port numbers

IP ACL commands can support ICMP even when it doesn't use port numbers. Instead, it uses a list of keywords to be matched against ICMP message types, or with the numeric message type and message code. Wildcard masks can be used to define a portion of the

IP address to examine. Each mask represent a 32-bit number, with binary 0s communicating that corresponding bits should be compared. Binary 1s are used to communicate the corresponding bits should be ignored. Given these points, some ample wild cards are:

- 0.0.0.0 – the entire IP address must match.
- 0.0.0.225 – the first 24 bits must match.
- 0.0.255.255 – the first 16 bits must match.
- 0.255.255.255 – the first 8 bits must match.
- 255.255.255.255 – all IP addresses are automatically considered.
- 0.0.7.255 – the first 21 bits must match.
- 15.78.128.3 – all bits are compared except 5, 6, 7, 8, 10, 13, 14, 15, 17, 31, and 32.

3.9.3 Security Considerations

When a host sends a large number of ICMP Echo Requests with some atypical IP address in the packet, the occurrence is a smurf attack. The destination addresses in these packets are called subnet broadcast address or directed broadcast address. They are forwarded by routers based on normal matching with the IP routing table until they reach the router connected to the destination subnet, where it is forwarded into the LAN as a broadcast packet. At the same time the source IP address of the attack packet is the IP address of the attacked host. As a result when hosts receive the broadcast message, they will reply with an Echo Reply to the source address of the original ICMP Echo. As a result the source IP address will potentially receive a large number of packets.

A Reverse-Path-Forwarding (RPF) check enables the Cisco IOS to examine the source IP address of the incoming packets on the interface. The interface command, ip verify unicast source reachable-via [rx|any][allow-default][allow-self-ping][*list*], is used to enable the RPF check. The check has two styles:

- Strict RPF – with the rx keyword, the outgoing interface of the matching route is checked to determine that it is the same interface the packet was received and discarded if they are not the same.
- Loose RPF – with the any keyword, any route is checks to determine if the source IP address can be reached.

The allow-default keyword allows default routes to be used when performing the check, and ignored when the keyword is not used.

3.9.4 TCP SYN Floods

When a large number of TCP connections are initiated but not completed, the server is suffering from a TCP SYN flood attack. The attacker is initiating TCP connections with only the TCP SYN flag set. The server will send a reply to finish the connection, but the attacker doesn't return the expected third message in the flow. As a result the server consumes memory and resources while waiting on timeouts to occur.

Stateful firewalls can prevent TCP SYN attacks. Another method is to filter all packets whose TCP header shows only the SYN flag set. The established keyword can be used to match TCP segments with the ACK flag set. This works well for clients outside of a network who are not allowed to make TCP connections into the network. TCP intercept is a feature of Cisco IOS can allow TCP connections into the network and monitor those connections for TCP SYN attacks.

TCP intercept has two modes of operations: watch and intercept. In watch mode, state information about the TCP connection is kept if it matches a defined ACL. If the three-way handshake is not completed within the specified time period, a TCP reset is sent to the server and counts the number of new connections attempted over time. If a large number of connections (default 1100) are attempted within 1 second, new TCP requests are filtered out. In intercept mode, TCP connection requests are replied to by the router instead of forwarded to the actual server. If the three-way handshake completes, the route create a TCP connection between the router and server and knits the two connections together.

3.9.5 Context-Based Access Control

Context-Based Access Control (CBAC) is a firewall feature that performs dynamic inspection of traffic that is explicitly specified and allowed to traverse a firewall router. This is based on actual protocol commands. CBAC determines what traffic is allowed to cross the firewall. If a session initiated is found on a trusted network for a protocol that would be blocked on other filtering methods, CBAC will create a temporary opening in the firewall to allow the inbound traffic from the untrusted network.

CBAC works on TCP and UDP traffic. The configurations possible in the CBAC are:

- Protocols to inspection.
- Interfaces to perform inspection on.
- Direction of the traffic to inspect for each interface.

The protocols that can be inspected by CBAC include:

- Any generic TCP session
- All UDP "sessions"
- FTP
- SMTP
- TFTP
- H.323
- Java
- CU-SeeMe
- Unix Commands
- RealAudio
- Sun RPC
- SQL*Net
- StreamWorks
- VDOLive

The limitations of CBAC include:

- If an access list blocks a type of traffic before it reaches the CBAC for inspection of inbound traffic, CBAC will never see the traffic.
- Attacks that originate within the network will not be protected by CBAC.
- Only the protocols specified will be inspected by CBAC, leaving all other filtering to access lists and other methods.
- Only TCP and UDP transported traffic is inspected by CBAC.
- Only the traffic traversing the firewall is inspected, not traffic sent to or from the firewall will be inspected by CBAC.
- Encrypted traffic has some restrictions in CBAC.

To configure CBAC:

A) Choose an interface.
B) Configure an IP access list for the interface.
C) Configure global timeouts and thresholds with the ip inspect commands.
D) Define an inspection rule and optional rule-specific timeout value using the ip inspects name *protocol* command.
E) Apply inspection rules to an interface.

3.9.6 Dynamic Multipoint VPN

IPSec, GRE tunnels, and Next Hop resolution Protocol are used by Dynamic Multipoint VPN (DMVPM to enable greater scalability for IP Sec in hub and spoke networks. It also allows traffic segmentation across VPN, as well as being VRF aware. When using DMVPN, the hub router is configured for a single multipoint GRE tunnel interface and a set of profiles for the spoke routers, rather than being explicitly configured with the spoke router connection information. Each spoke router will point to one or more hubs to enable better redundancy and load balancing.

The benefits of DMVPN over a traditional hub and spoke VPN environment are:

- Simpler hub router configuration with one multipoint GRE tunnel interface, one IPSec profile, and no crypto access list.
- Zero-touch at the hub router for provisioned spoke routers.
- Automatically initiated IPSec encryption.
- Dynamic addressing support for spoke routers.
- Dynamically created spoke-to-spoke tunnels.
- VRF integration for MPLS environments.

3.9.7 Permitting and Denying Access

By default, all traffic from a higher security interface to a lower security interface is automatically allowed. Access lists can be used to filter this traffic even more, or to allow traffic to travel from a lower security interface to a higher security interface. In this sense, access lists come in two types to control traffic:

- Inbound – applied to traffic as it enters an interface.
- Outbound – applied to traffic as it exits an interface.

Access control is supported in single and multiple context mode, as well as routed and transparent firewall modes. When in transparent modes, extended access lists are used to control Layer 3 traffic while EtherType access lists are used to control Layer 2 traffic.

To control traffic which is using connectionless protocols, the access lists must be applied to both the source and destination interfaces to control the traffic in both directions.

When packets arrive at a firewall, a per-user access list is identified and applied first. If no such access lists exists, the interface access list is applied. A per-user access list has a specified timeout value, which can be overridden by the AAA per-user session timeout value.

3.9.8 Authentication, Authorization, and Accounting

AAA is a term applied to Authentication, Authorization, and Accounting and refers to a number of common security features. Authentication is the process for managing access to a router or IOS switch. It applies to both user mode and privilege mode. The strongest authentication method is using TACACS+ or RADIUS server, though other type of AAA server can be used, including:

- RSA/SDI
- NT-Server
- Kerberos
- LDAP
- SSO for Clientless SSL VPN
- Local databases

The server will than compare the username and password with entries in the system and if a match exists; communicate back to the router or switch the appropriate acceptance. If no match exists, the communication specifies that no access should be granted.

A single authentication method is a way to authenticate a user. This can be done by using a RADIUS server or having the router look at a locally defined username commands. The simplest AAA configuration defines a default set of authentication methods for all router and switch logins. A second set of default authentication methods are used by the enable command.

AAA authentication can reference multiple servers or multiple authentication methods. This is done to ensure that the user can be authenticated even if one authentication method is not working. Up to four methods can be supported on a single AAA authentication command. As for the number of RADIUS or TACACS+ servers, there is no limit. An ordered list of authentication methods can be configured: authentication will process through each method in order on the list until an' accept' or 'reject' for the user is returned.

3.9.9 Network Access Translation

RFC 1631 defines Network Access Translation, which allows organizations to use private IP address on an internal network and the Internet at the same time. This is done by using a valid registered IP address to represent the private address on the Internet.

Several variations of NAT are supported:

- Static NAT
- Dynamic NAT
- Overloading NAT with Port Address Translation (PAT)

With Static NAT, the IP addresses are statically mapped to each other, creating a one-to-one relationship between the registered address and the private address.

With Dynamic NAT, the one-to-one relationship between the registered address and the private address still exists. The registered addresses, or global addresses, are part of a pool of IP addresses which are dynamically used. Dynamic NAT defines criteria for determining how private addresses, or local addresses, should be translated.

With Dynamic NAT, an organization can have more local addresses than global addresses. When a packet arrives that needs a NAT entry, a global address is retrieved from the pool and associated to the local address. If no global address is available, the packet is discarded.

Overloading allows NAT to support clients with a few global addresses. Port Address Translation (PAT) will translate the port number in addition to the IP address. With dynamic mapping, NAT provides a global IP address, but also a unique port number associated with that address. The NAT router keeps a table entry for every unique combination of local addresses and ports. With a 16-bit field for port numbers, overloading NAT provides more than 65,000 port numbers.

Though an organization has access to private addresses registered to them, they can also utilize network numbers registered to another organization. NAT will translate the source and destination IP addresses of two organizations using a network number if they are connected to the Internet. As the packet passes through the NAT router, the source and destination addresses are changed.

3.9.10 Policy NAT

Extended access lists can be used to specify source and destination addresses for address translation. This method is the basis for Policy NAT. Normally, NAT will only consider the source address; but with Policy NAT, the destination address can also be given a mapped address. When applications require inspection for secondary channels, the policy statement in policy NAT should include the secondary ports. When ports cannot be predicted, only IP address for the secondary channel should be specified by the policy.

4. XenApp

4.1 Management Tools

4.1.1 Access Management Console

A number of management functions are performed through the Access Management Console. It can be snapped into the Microsoft Management Console (MMC) in Windows Server 2008. The functions of this console include:

- Managing items administered by other Citrix products.
- Set up and monitor servers, server farms, published resources, and sessions.
- Create reports.
- Configure application access.
- Diagnose problems and troubleshoot alerts.
- View hotflix information
- Setup health checks
- Track administrative changes

The Access Management Console can be accessed through the Start menu. One of the first operations to be performed when opening the console is to identify the devices and applications that were added or removed from the environment. When the console is opened for the first time, an automated prompt is made to initiate the process of discovery, which allows the administrator to select the components to look for, configuring the process, and finding the items to manage.

After this initial step, the discovery process can be initiated whenever a new item has been added or removed from the environment or to configure discovery for a component. When using discovery, at least one server in each farm being managed must have its name or IP address specified.

4.1.2 Custom Administrators

When a installing the first server within a server farm, the credentials for a full authority Citrix administrator must be provided. The account for this administrator will be provided the authority to manage and administrate over the entire server farm. This is the account that is used to open the Access Management console and add other administrators.

Custom administrators can be created and grant privileges for different levels of access to areas of the server farm management. This required since only Citrix administrators can use the Access management Console to manage the server farms. To set administrator privileges, go to the left pane of the Access Management Console and select the Farm node, then Action > New > Add administrator. This will open the Add Citrix Administrator wizard where privileges can be granted to specified administrators. It is recommended to use domain accounts to run Access Management Console.

Administrators with the proper authority can perform:

- Display Customizing
- Manage applications and servers in multiple server farms
- View zones, or configurable groups of XenApp servers
- Manage User Sessions and Server Processes
- Create Reports
- Configure Application Access
- Create Trace Logs
- View Hotfix Information
- Conserving Bandwidth

4.1.3 XenApp Advanced Configuration

Policies and printers can be set up within any server farm using the XenApp Advanced Configuration Tool. Only Citrix administrators can use the Advanced Configuration tool. A specific administrator may have varying levels of access to perform server farm management. If an administrator does not have the proper access, the details pane of the tool will not display the related information.

The Advanced Configuratin tool is installed on each server in the farm by XenApp Setup. To install the tool on other workstations, the XenApp installation media should be used.

4.1.4 Citrix Relay Configuration Tool

The Relay Configuration Tool can be used to secure the communication between a server running the Web Interface and a server farm.

4.1.5 Shadow Taskbar

Users' session can be remotely viewed and controlled using a technique called shadowing. The Shadow Taskbar can be used to establish these shadow sessions and switch between multiple shadowed sessions.

4.1.6 SpeedScreen Latency Reduction Manager

To improve user experience on slow networks, the SpeedScreen Latency Reduction Manager can be used.

4.2 Licensing Architecture

In order to use any Citrix Product, a system of various components called Citrix Licensing must be installed. The components of this system include:

- License server - allows licenses to the shared on the network.

- License files - required to license a product and stored on the license server.
- Console - the interface used to manage the license server and the license files stored on it.
- Product setting - configuration within the Citrix products which are associated with the license server.

4.2.1 Citrix Licensing

Every Citrix environment must have at least one license server. This server can be dedicated to storing and management licenses or shared to perform other functions within the environment. Licenses stored on the license server are requested by Citrix products when users attempt to connect to the servers containing those products.

License files associated with the product must be stored on the license server. The product must be configured to communicate with the license server where the licenses are located. Since licensing functions can be installed on a server shared with other application, a single dedicated license server, or as part of multiple license servers, the configuration must be associated with the specific server that contains the licenses. To manage and monitor licenses, the License Administration Console provides a user interface to the license server, which provides dashboards of license and alerts, manage license files and license server settings.

4.2.2 License Process

When a Citrix product is started, a connection is opened to the license server using a startup license which is checked out from the license server. This startup license is a Citrix system file which enables a continuous connection between the server and the product. A license server can support up to 4000 continuous connections.

When a user first connects to a Citrix product, a license is requested by the product on behalf of the user. This request goes to the license server. The license server will grant the license request to the Citrix product and the product will reserve the use of the license in a process called checking out the license. When the user disconnects from the product, the license is returned to the license server in a process called checking in. A license is checked out for a predetermined time period.

A replica of the licensing information is stored by the Citrix product, which includes the number and type of licenses. This replica is in place in case the connection with the license server is lost. When this happens, a grace period is entered and the product will use the local replica to provide licenses to users. The grace period is set by Citrix and is typically 30 days, but can vary from product to product. The grace period is entered when the connection is lost. This is determined when "heartbeat" messages which are sent between the product and license servers every five minutes fail to be sent or received. If the grace period expires, no connections are accepted by the product. Once the connection between the product and license server is reestablished, the grace period is reset.

4.2.3 License Server

Several components make up the license server:

- Citrix vendor daemon – using TCP/IP on port 7279, this process runs on the server to grant licenses and tracks the number of licenses checked out and by what products.
- Console – interface to manage and monitor licenses.
- License files – text files which store licensing information for products and are used to determine whether licenses should be granted to a product.
- Options file – a configuration file of the license server which defines the behavior around the licensing process, including the number of license used, the location of system logs, and other user-defined customizations.
- Startup license – allows Citrix products to communicate with the license server to open a continuous connection. The startup license contains information about which product servers are connected to the license server and the licensing system itself.

4.2.4 License Types

There are several types of licenses that can be checked out. Most products will allow only one type of license to be chosen, though some allow multiple types. The types of licenses are:

- User or device licenses – used by XenDesktop 4 to allow licenses to be assigned to a user or device to provide access to an unlimited number of devices or users. A unique device ID is required to license a device. A licensed device is authorized to be used by individuals to access an instance of XenDesktop and is often used for shared devices. To license a user, a unique user ID is required. Database solutions such as Active Directory can be leveraged to provide user information. When a license is assigned to a user, they can access multiple instances of XenDesktop and applications through multiple devices.
- Concurrent user licenses – checked out to the device used by the user and not specifically assigned to the user. Once the users logs off from a session with a product, the license is checked in and available for another user.
- Concurrent system licenses – checked out to a system, such as an operating system or virtual machine instance, and checked in when the system is no longer running. One license is required for each system running.
- Named user licenses – checked out to the user, rather than a device or system, and allows the user to run

multiple sessions on different computers without additional licenses needing to be checked out.

4.2.5 License Administration Console

To manage and monitor Citrix Licenses, the License Administration Console can be used through a Web browser. The Dashboard portion of the console allows licenses to be monitored, how they are used, and any associated alerts. Within the Administration area of the console, the following tasks are possible:

- Administering licenses
- Configuring console users
- Configuring alerts
- Importing licenses
- Logging license management activities
- Securing the console server
- Viewing system information

The License Administration Console can be opened from the Start menu on the machine it is installed. To open the console from a remote location, to one of the following URL options:

- http:// license server name:webservice port
- http:// cluster name:web service port
- http:// IP:web service port

    where

license server name represents the name of the license server.

cluster name represents the name of the cluster containing the license server.

IP represents the IP address of the license server.

web service port represents the port number for the Web service of the console: default being 8082.

4.2.6 License Reporting

Licensing activity can be logged into a report. These reports can allow a person to understand the rate of consumptions for licenses in the environment. Report logging is inactive by default. To enable report logging:

- Go to License Management Console.
- Click on Configure License Server.
- Click File Locations.
- Click Change under Report Log.
- Enter the path where the report log should be created and provide a meaningful name to the report. An .rl extension must be part of the name.
- Click Change to create the report log.

The log will now appear in the License Management Console.

Historical reports provide information about past license activities to view availability and consumptions of the licenses over time. Through the License Management Console, the report can focus on the type of product, date range, summary period, and data types used in the report. The summary period refers to the amount of data group together in the chart, by day, week, month, and so on. The information contains in the historical reports are found in the report logs.

To generate a report for a product or a summary report, the following process is used:

- Click Historical Usage.
- Click Add.
- From the Available Report Logs list, choose one or more report logs to be used in the report.
- Click Add.
- Click one of the following:
- Product Reports
- Summary Reports
- Choose the report settings for the report.
- Click Generate Report.

To generate a report for a user, the following process is used:

- Click Historical Usage.
- Click Add.
- From the Available Report Logs list, choose one or more report logs to be used in the report.
- Click Add.
- Click User Reports.
- Choose the product license and dates.

- Click Proceed with Selected Product and Date Range.
- Click Generate Unique User List for Selected Product and Date Range.
- To close the user list, click Close.
- From the Generate User Reports screen, click Edit List.
- Choose the users to contain in the report and click Add Selected.
- Click Submit.
- Choose the summary period for the report.
- Choose the type of data to be contained in the report, including:
- Peak Count.
- License Usage Time.
- Click Generate Report.

4.3 Citrix Administrator Accounts

Individuals responsible for managing and administering server farms are called Citrix administrators. It is possible to associate any member of a Windows or Novell Directory Services account authority as a Citrix administrator. The scope of authority for different administrators can be customized. This is done by assigning different tasks to individuals or groups of individuals.

4.3.1 Types of Administrator Accounts

Administrator accounts can be created and configured with three different levels of authority:

- Full Authority – can manage all aspects of the server farm.
- View-only Authority – can view all aspects of the server farm but cannot modify any settings.
- Custom Authority – can performed a select set of tasks and may have mixed levels of access across the different aspects of server farms, ranging from view-only, write, or no access.

The granted access of an administrator is dependent on the business function responsibilities of that administrator. To create an administrator account:

- Open the Access Management console.
- Select a farm.
- Select Action > New > Add Administrator.
- Select the name of the user or group to designate as Citrix Administrator.
- Click Add.
- Select the authority level of grant from the Privileges page.

When creating a customer administrator, use the Tasks pane to select the delegated tasks.

Access for an administrator can be temporarily removed by disabling the associated Citrix administrator accounts. An account can also be completely removed for events such as personnel changes. Only administrators with full authority can disable or remove accounts. These actions can be performed in the Administrators node of the Access Management Console.

4.3.2 Delegating Tasks

Custom administrators can be provided permissions to perform specific tasks. This is done through the Access Management Console. Windows, Active Directory, or NDS groups can be used to assign permissions. This will allow users to be added and removed from the groups without having to change the permissions provided. Set permissions on nodes are applied across the entire farm, while permissions on folders are applied to servers and applications contained within a folder. Permission cannot be directly granted to servers and applications.

From the Access Management Console, go to select the administrator to delegate a task. From the task option, select Modify Administrator Properties. This will open a list of folders. Select the folder to grant access. From the task pane, click Permissions under the Other Task options. Associate existing administrators to the folder or create new administrators.

Use the Advanced Configuration tool to view and assign permissions on specific objects. Object permissions must be done by Citrix administrators with full authority. From the console, select the appropriate farm and select Set permission on objects under the Other Tasks option in the task pane.

4.4 Resources

Citrix solutions based on XenAPP provide a variety of virtualized resources, such as:

- Applications – applications installed on servers but appear as if running locally on client devices.
- Streamed Applications – stored on a file server and installed in application profiles, these applications are virtualized on the client desktop when users access the profile.
- Data files – files that make up the content of applications and includes Web pages, documents, media files, spreadsheets, and URLs.
- Server Desktops – enables access to all resources on the server.

4.4.1 Accessing Resources

The Publish Application wizard is used to provide access to a common set of resources to different types of client devices. Users can access these resources from the server. The name of the server is not required to access these resources.

When an application is published, its configuration information is stored in the data store in the server farm. This information includes the types of files used by the application, the users who connect to the application, the application's importance level within the Preferential Load Balancing function, and the properties for client-size sessions.

When a user accesses an application, they appear similar to applications installed locally on the client device. How the applications are started is dependent on the plugin running on the client device.

4.4.2 Installing Applications

Before an application is installed on a server, the Terminal Services configuration in Windows Server 2008 must be enabled. XenApp does not need to be installed to install applications for publications. In Windows Server 2008, the User Account Control (UAC) can affect how applications are installed for publication. Multiple users will not be able to connect to a published application simultaneously unless the application is installed for all users. To enable applications to be used by multiple users, install the applications using the following methods:

- In the installation wizard, select an "install for multiple users" option.
- Install application as the Built-in Administrator.
- Use the command line.

When publishing applications for directory services or domain environment like Microsoft Active Directory Service, the recommendation from Citrix is:

- Assign and categorize permissions using groups.
- Add users through the Citrix User Selection using the Add List of Names options.

Published Resources have several delivery options through the Publish Application wizard and application properties, including:

- Selecting a resource type.
- Configuring different options:
    - Locations
    - User access
    - Shortcuts
    - Access Control
    - Content redirection
    - Application limits
    - Client options
    - Application appearance
    - Application importance

- User privileges

4.4.3 Selecting Resource Types

Resource types are initially selected in the Publish Application wizard under the Action menu. The resource types available are server desktop, content, and application.

The server desktop will publish the entire Windows desktop of a server from the farm. A plugin will connect to the server. Once the connection is made, the user will see the desktop interface where any application installed on the server can be selected. XenApp is required to publish a desktop.

Nonexecutable information called content can be published. To do so, a Uniform Resource Locator (URL) or Universal Naming Convention (UNC) path to the file must be specified. Content represents:

- Web site addresses
- Document file on Web server
- Directory on FTP server
- Document file on a FTP server
- UNC file path
- UNC directory path

Applications can be installed on one or more servers within the server farm. If a computer running the console is not a member of the farm, the application cannot be published to that farm. Published applications come in several varieties that must be specified:

- Server Access Only – applications run on a XenApp server and uses shared server resources. The location of the executable files and the XenApp server must be specified.
- Streamed Only - the application is profiled and streams from a file share to the client device. The application launches locally and uses client resources rather than server resources. The XenApp Plugin for Streamed Apps must be installed and access an application using the XenApp Plugin for Hosted Apps or a Web interface site. If a client does not support streamed application, the client will not launch the application.
- Streamed or Server Access – also called dual mode streaming, the application is accessed through the profile and streamed to the client device. If a client device does not support streamed applications, an ICA connection can be used to access the application from the XenApp server.

4.4.4 User Access

From the Publish Application wizard, select the Users page to choose the user accounts which should have access to the application. This can also be done from within the application's properties by selecting Actions. The configuration of the user accounts can affect their access. Anonymous users will allow all users to log on anonymously and start the streamed application without a user name. Configured users will only allow those users who have been explicitly granted access to start the application.

The Anonymous user group is created during the installation of XenApp. Applications published for this user group required no authentication for use, and therefore, has no username or password requirement. The minimal session permissions are granted to anonymous users with the following restrictions:

- After ten minutes of inactivity, user time-outs.
- Time outs and broken connection will result in logoff from the application.
- Passwords are not required and cannot be changed.

Any user who is not part of the anonymous groups is considered an explicit user. These users have user accounts that can be created, configured, and maintained using any standard user account management tool. Some limitations exist for explicit users when they run applications from a server farm. Administrators can specify the type of profile, settings, and other configuration which apply for these users.

4.4.5 Content Redirection

Content redirection refers to the capability to redirect the application and content launching from the server to the client or from the client to the server. The capability enables how information is accessed with applications published on the server or application running locally on the client device to be determined.

When content redirection from client to server is configured, a user running the XenApp Plugin for Hosted Apps will open all files of the associated type with applications on the server. Client to server content redirection is only available to users connecting with Citrix XenApp. The Web interface server must be configured to allow users to connect to applications and will update Citrix XenApp with properties from published applications. If users run applications locally, the content redirection capability will redirect applications launching from the client device to the server. Content which the user attempts to access, such as an attachment in an email, will open an application published on the server which is associated with the file type of the content and is assigned to the user.

When content redirection from server to client is configured, the XenApp server will intercept embedded URLs and send to the client device. The URL will be displayed or played on the locally installed browser on the client device. The URL types opened locally on client devices through content redirection are:

- HyperText Transfer Protocol (HTTP)

- Secure Hypertext Transfer Protocol (HTTPS)
- Real Player and QuickTime (RTSP)
- Real Player and QuickTime (RTSPU)
- Legacy Real Player (PNM)
- Microsoft Media Format (MMS)

When users are allowed to open published content with locally running applications, the client will pass the name of the published content file to the local viewer application. The file is not downloaded from the server to the client. The local viewer application will access the file from the server. This process does not use XenApp resources or licenses because the local viewer applications do not use ICA sessions to display the content.

When applications are published, they are associated to certain file types which are present in the Windows registry on the server. The initial associations are made with the Publish Application wizard and later within application properties. Associations enable the content publishing and content redirection automatically.

4.4.6 Limits and Importance

When starting a published application, the connection is established with the server and a session is initiated. If a second published application is started without logging off from the first application, another connection is created. The user now has two concurrent connections to the server farm. The number of concurrent connections be limited through the Publish Application wizard or application properties. In application properties, go the Action menu and select modify application properties. Keep moving through the options: Modify all properties > Advanced > Limits until the Concurrent instances configurations can be seen.

Application importance refers to the configurable settings which determine how much server resources will be dedicated to an application session. This importance is determined by the Preferential Load Balancing setting and the session importance policy setting and affects the Resource Allotment. The higher the Resource Allotment, the higher the percentage of CPU cycles allotted to the resource will be. The setting is configured in the Publish Application wizard or within the application properties. Use the same path as concurrent connections until the priority can be set for Session Importance under Application Importance.

4.4.7 Managing Applications

Applications can be renamed, moved, disabled, and deleted. Settings within published applications can be changed, duplicated, imported, and exported. This can all be performed by a Citrix administrator with full authority to the Published Application task. After using the Publish Application wizard to install and publish the application, any additional management of the application is performed within the application's properties.

4.4.8 Virtual IP Addresses

A unique IP address is required by some applications published. Some application required the address or a loopback address because it has capabilities dependent on addressing, licensing, identification, or such. Some applications bind to a static port, which if already used, will cause attempts by multiple users to access the application to fail. The Virtual IP address feature allows a static range of IP addresses to a server to be assigned and allocated individually to each session. This will allow applications to appear to have a unique IP address. This feature will allow applications which depend on communications with localhost to use a unique virtual loopback addresses.

The processes which require a unique virtual IP either have a hard-coded TCP port number or they use Windows sockets and require a unique IP address or specified TCP port number. Processes which require a Virtual loopback address either uses a hard-coded TCP port number or uses the Windows socket loopback address. Virtual addresses work by:

- The virtual IP address assigner will bind an assigned IP address to the Network Interface Card during IMA startup. The assigned IP address will match the same subnet of the virtual address.
- The virtual IP address allocator will allocate an address to all new sessions when the feature is enabled on a specific

server. The address comes from a pool of available addresses assigned by the virtual IP address assigner.

- The address allocated to a new session is removed from the pool of addresses and returned to the pool when the session ends.
- When an IP address is allocated to a session, the allocated addresses is used rather than the primary IP address for the system whenever the specific calls are made. Those calls are:
    - bind
    - closesocket
    - connect
    - WSACccept
    - getpeername
    - getsockname
    - sendto
    - WSASendTo
    - WSASocketW
    - gethostbyname
    - gethostbyaddr
    - getnameinfo
    - getaddrinfo

Virtual loopback requires that the processes which use the feature be specified. No additional configuration is required. When enabled, an application using the localhost address (127.0.0.1) will be replaced with 127.X.X.X where X.X.X represents the session ID plus 1. Multiple published applications which require a localhost interface will work properly when the virtual loopback feature is enabled.

Applications can be bound to specific IP addresses by inserting a component between the application and Winsock function calls which identifies only the IP address the application is supposed to use. When the application listens for TCP or UDP communications, it is bound to the allocated virtual IP address automatically. Any connection opened by the application utilizes the IP address bound to the application. Sometimes an application will want to bind to a port for listening on the address 0.0.0.0. When this happens, only on instance of the application can be launched. The Virtual IP address feature will change the call to listen on a specific virtual IP address and perform the listening on the port. This allows multiple instances of the application to be launched, since the application is listening to different virtual IP addresses on the same port.

4.5 Policies

Policies are used in XenApp to control connection, security, and bandwidth considerations attributed to user access and the session environment. They can be created for specific groups of users, devices, or connection types. An individual policy may contain multiple rules ranging in broad scope such as:

- Controlling quality of sound.
- Allowing access to specific folders on a local client device.
- Routing print jobs.

- Set encryption levels.
- Redirecting server connections in the event of server disruption.
- Setting the importance level of a session.

Multiple policies can be prioritized to determine precedence when a conflict between policies occurs. When using a Citrix product, the policies of the product will always be taken over policies and settings already in place in the environment, including Activity Directory and Windows settings.

4.5.1 Configuring Policies

To configure policies in XenApp, the following process is used:

- Create the policy
- Name the policy
- Apply policy rules
- Apply the policy to connections for filtering
- Prioritize the policy

The policies set for XenApp will override any similar settings that have been configured for the entire server farm, specific servers, or the client. The one exception to this general rule is encryption and shadowing setting, which will take the most restrictive policy in place. XenApp policies only apply to open connections to the server farms and will remain open as long as the session continued. If policy changes are made while users are connected to the server farm, those policies will not take effect until the next session for the user.

4.5.2 Creating Policies

When creating a policy, be mindful to the group of users or devices which the policy will be applied. If a policy is created for the group, it may be better to change the existing policy, rather than create a new policy. Policies may be created to focus on user job functions, connection types, client devices, or geographic location or they may take on the same criteria found in Active Directory policies.

The Advanced Configuration tool is used to create a policy. The steps are:

- Select Policies in the left pane.
- Select Actions > New > Policy.
- Enter the name of the policy and description.
- If using preconfigured rules for the policy, select Optimize initial policy settings for a connection type.
- Select the connection type from the drop-down list. Choices are WAN, Satellite, and Dial-up.

The rules found in policies define and configure the connection settings to be applied. Rules can be enabled, disabled, or not configured. To be applied, the policies must be enabled. By default, they are not configured. To configure a policy rule, select the policy in the Advanced Configuration tool and go into its properties from the

Action menu. The rules that can be applied are inside folders which need to be expanded. Policy rules fall into three states:

- Not configured – the default setting which has rules being ignored but will be embedded in a lower ranked policy.
- Enabled – adds the rule to the policy and allows the rule options to be set.
- Disabled – disallows the rule and prevents it from embedded in a lower ranked policy.

4.5.3 Applying Policies

A filter must be created for a server to apply a policy to matching connections. Filters can be created using any combination of the criteria below:

- IP address of the connecting client device
- Name of the connecting client device
- User or group membership
- Hosting server
- Access control

At least one filter must be added to apply a policy, although multiple filters can be used. A policy will apply only to those connections meeting all the filters. When a user logs on, all matching policies for the connection are identified. The policies are sorted by XenApp by priority. Multiple instances of any rule are compared and the rule with the highest priority is applied. Any rule that is disabled will take precedence over any lower ranked rule that is enabled. Any policy that is not configured is ignored.

To add a filter:

- Select Policies in the Advanced Configuration tool.
- Select the policy to apply from the Contents tab.
- Use the Actions menu to choose Policy, than Apply this policy to.
- In the Policy Filters dialog box, select a filter for policy based on access control, IP address, client name, servers, or users.
- Select Filter based on 'type of filter' to enable the policy filter.
- Repeat the steps to each filter applied.

4.5.4 Policy Management

Citrix recognizes the following best practices for managing initial policy rules:

- User policies should be assigned to group rather than individuals to allow automatic updating as users are added or removed from the group.
- Conflicting or overlapping settings should not be enabled in the Terminal Services Configuration tool or the Access Management console's settings for server farms.

- All unused policies should be disabled to reduce unnecessary processing.
- Unused policy rules should be set to Not Configured to allow the rule to be applied to lower ranked policies.

4.5.5 Multiple Policies

The use of multiple policies allows XenApp to be tailored to meet users' needs. When using multiple policies, possible conflicts should be considered. To handle appropriately, an effective policy should be in place, applied policies should be prioritized, and exceptions should be created. All policies associated to an application will take precedence over similar settings in the server farm, except security settings.

XenApp policies will also interact with the policies set in the operating system. The highest security policy will always take precedence. Citrix policies will always take precedence over Windows settings and policies. They are designed to work with Active Directory policies.

4.5.6 Prioritizing Policies

The policy with the highest priority will take precedence when a conflict occurs between policies. Policies are given different policy numbers. The default setting is the lowest policy number when a policy is created. The highest priority is 1. Rules are merged according to priority and the rule's state. A disabled rule will override a lower ranked rule that is enabled. Rules that are not configured will be ignored.

4.5.7 Exceptions

When policies are created for groups, some members of the group may require an exception to the policy rule. Exceptions are made by creating policies that are applied to the smaller subset of group members and ranking that policy higher than the original policy.

4.6 Server Farms

Server farms are groupings of servers which are managed as a single entity. They run Citrix XenApp and share a single IMA-based data store. All servers within the farm are managed through the Access Management Console and the XenApp Advanced Configuration tool.

4.6.1 Organizing the Farm

The properties found within a server on the farm are configurations which are specific to the individual server or the entire farm of servers. By default, all servers are configured to use the settings set for the entire farm. However, farm settings can be overridden for individual servers.

The configurations of the farm and individual servers can be viewed through the Access Management Console.

4.6.2 Scheduled Restarts

Performance within the farm can be improved by restarting servers automatically on specific intervals. Restart schedules rely on the local times of each server, preventing restarts from occurring simultaneously across a multi-geographic server farm. When a restart is performed, the Citrix Independent Management Architecture creates a connection with the data store to update the local host cache. The update can vary in size based on the size of the server farm.

4.6.3 Health Monitoring and Recovery

Health Monitoring and Recovery is a feature of the Enterprise and Platinum editions of XenApp and provides tests to monitor server states and identify any risks to the health of the servers on the farm. 10 tests are included in the feature:

- Terminal Services test – enumerates the list of sessions running on the server and the session user information.
- XML Service test – request a ticket for SML services running on the server and prints the ticket.
- Citrix IMA Service test – queries the IMA service by enumerating the applications available on the server.

- Logon Monitor test – monitors the session logon/logoff cycles to identify any problems with session initialization or possible application failures.
- Check DNS test – performs a forward DNS lookup using the local host name to query a local DNS server.
- Check Local Host Cache test – ensures the server's local host cache does not have corrupted data or duplicate entries.
- Check XML threads test – inspects the threshold of worker threads currently running in the Citrix XML Service.
- Citrix Print Manager Service test – enumerates session printers.
- Microsoft Print Spooler Service test – enumerates printer drivers, printer processors, and printers.
- ICA Listener test – determines the acceptability of ICA connections by a XenApp server.

4.6.4 Preferential Load Balancing

Importance levels can be assigned to specific users and applications. By default, all users and application are assigned a normal level of server. However, some users and applications may have critical importance to the business operations and have a heightened level. The assignment of these levels is done in a function called Preferential Load Balancing. The importance levels are calculated from the Resource Allotment for each session.

The Resource Allotment will determine importance levels for both the session and the published application. The policy engine for the session will impact the session result, which determines the level of service experienced by the session relative to other sessions on the same server and other servers within the server farms. The higher a session's Resource Allotment, the higher the service it experiences. Service represents the number of CPU cycles that are allotted to the session.

Importance can be set at High, Normal, or Low. Since importance is attributed to both the application and session, the importance levels are multiplied to obtain the session's Resource Allotment. There are up to six possible results for a session:

Application Importance X	Session Importance =	Resource Allotment
Low (1)	Low (1)	1
Low (1)	Normal (2)	2
Low (1)	High (3)	3
Normal (2)	Low (1)	2
Normal (2)	Normal (2)	4
Normal (2)	High (3)	6
High (3)	Low (1)	3
High (3)	Normal (2)	6
High (3)	High (3)	9

When multiple published applications are running in the same session, Resource Allotment is calculated on the maximum application importance settings of all the published applications running in the session. If a new application starts on an existing session, its importance level is compared with the importance levels of the applications currently running. If the importance level is higher, the Resource Allotment for the session is recalculated. When an application closes within a session, a comparison is made again and if the remaining applications have a lower importance then the closing application, the Resource Allotment is recalculated and lowered for the remaining applications.

4.6.5 Farm Infrastructure

All farms are comprised by at least one zone, or grouping of servers. Geographically segmented farms may be comprised of multiple zones to improve performance. Each zone has a data collector which contains information about the other servers residing on the farm. Other servers may be designated as backup data collectors. If the data store should fail, each server contains a backup of the data store in a local host cache.

The local host cache can include the entire data store or, most likely, a subset of information in the data store. When a change is made to the data store of the farm, a notification is sent to all servers in the farm to update their respective local host caches. Servers will also query the data store regularly to identify any changes in the data store and request the changed information if changes have been made. The default interval for querying the data store is 30 minutes.

4.6.6 Data Collectors

A data collector is a database maintaining dynamic information about the servers within a zone. This information can include data about server loads, session status, published applications, connected users, and license usage. Incremental data updates are received by the data collector and servers within the zone will make queries on the information collected by the data collector. Information from one data collector is relayed to other data collectors on the farm and the data store, alleviating the need for individual servers to communicate information to these places.

The determination of the data collector in a farm is based on the election preference for the server. All servers joining the farm will default to a default backup data collector. If the primary data collector fails, an election occurs to determine the new data collector. Existing and incoming sessions are not affected by a data collector election. The election preference can be configured with one of four options:

- Most Preferred
- Preferred
- Default Preference
- Not Preferred

4.6.7 Zones

All farms have at least one zone. All servers must belong to a zone. All servers in the farm belong, by default, to the same zone, called the Default zone. Multiple zones can improve performance by grouping geographically related servers. There are two purposes for zones:

- Collecting data from servers in a hierarchical structure.
- Efficient distribution of changes to all servers in a farm.

Each zone has a dedicated data collector containing all information about a zone's servers and published applications. Data collectors from different zones will communicate with each other and act as gateways for information across the farm.

4.7 Session Environments

A session is the particular instance of activity on the server by a user, creating a virtualization of the user's environment. The session begins when the user connected to the server farm and opens a published application. The server then opens the application within a session. The session ends when the user disconnects from the server farm usually by closing the application.

Connections are the links between the user's client device and the server within the farm. Through these connections, users are able to access published content within the session. Administrators can customize the connections and session environments.

4.7.1 Understanding Sessions

When a user starts an application, the client devices will make a connection to a server on the server farm. When this connection is completed, the server launches the application and the session is initiated. During the session, the user interacts with the application as if it was launched from the local computer. If the session disconnects, the application continues to run on the server until it is closed by the user. The application's session is ended by exiting the application and logging off the server. If the application is not exited before logging off, the session remains active. The session will remain active for the user to reconnect to the server from either the original client device or on another device.

4.7.2 User Environments

The experience the user has within a session can be controlled and customized. The available options for customization are:

- Suppressing the number of progress bars seen when opening an application to make the process more seamless.
- Allowing or preventing users from accessing local drives or ports during a session.
- Allowing or preventing users from hearing audio or using microphones during a session.

- Ensuring access to appropriate printers and devices to remote users during a session.
- The appearance of applications and desktops in a Remote Desktop window or seamless with the operating system.

4.7.3 User Logons

When connecting to a server, all the connection and logon status information appears by default in a series of screens from the Windows operating system. The user sees all these screens during the authentication process between the client and the server until the published application launches on the clients desktop.

These screens can be suppressed to make the process appear more seamless to the user; making them feel like they are opening an application locally rather than from a server. This suppression is performed by enabling through XenApp Setup the following local group policies on the server with the installed product:

- Administrative Templates > System > Remove > Remove Boot / Shutdown / Logon / Logoff status messages
- Administrative Templates > System > Verbose versus normal status messages

Active Directory group policies will take precedence over any equivalent Windows local group policies on the servers. If the server with the published application resides within an Active Directory domain, the Active Directory policies may prevent this suppression.

To prevent this, do not create the group policies in Active Directory which would prevent this suppression.

4.7.4 Controlling Access

With the Citrix XenApp Plugin for Hosted Apps, devices on the client computers can be mapped appropriately to allow access to those devices during the session; specifically allowing:

- Access to local drives and ports.
- Cut and paste data transfers between the session and the local clipboard.
- Audio playback.

The plugin will communicate to the server all the available client devices and COM ports during the logon process. The default mapping of client drives are to server drives to appear like there is a direct connection to the server. These mappings also appear as shared folders with mapped drive letters. The mappings are only available to the current user in the current session and are deleted when the session ends. The next time the user connects using this application, the mappings are recreated.

Usually, XenApp will try to map these drives according to clients' current drive letter configuration to allow similar access perspectives between local use and session use. Different drive letters will be mapped in the event the same drive letter is already in use on the server. The choice of drive letter starts with V and ascends until an unassigned drive letter is found.

Client drive mapping can be turned off through the policies configured in XenApp. Specific mappings to client drives can also be turned off. If a specific drive is not required during the session, it is recommended to disable access to the drive to make the logon process faster. By default, XenApp client drives are mapped without “user execute” permission. This default must be overridden before users can execute files located on the client drives. To override the default, the value of ExecuteFromMappedDrive must be edited in the registry on a XenApp server.

In addition to mapping drives, XenApp allows COM port mappings to be performed. These mappings allow access to devices attached to COM ports from remote applications running on the server. There is no automatic mapping performed during logon. To manually map ports, use the net use or CHGCDM commands.

To allow applications running on the server to play sounds through a client device, client audio mappings must be in place. The server can control the amount of bandwidth used in client audio mappings. Citrix policies are used to create client audio mappings.

4.7.5 Special Folders

Special Folders Redirection allows users to save files to special folders on their local drive. “Special folders” is a Microsoft term referring to standard folders in the Windows operating system such as Documents (My Documents), Computer (My Computer), and Desktop. Without the redirection, the Documents and Desktop icons which appear within a session to the user will represent the Documents and Desktop folders on the server and reserved for the user. The Special Folders Redirection will change the representation of these icons to those located on the user’s local computer. It will also redirect the Document folder in the Start menu for the Citrix XenApp plugin.

The Special Folders Redirection is only available to those users connecting to the server farm using Citrix XenApp Plugin 1.1 or the Web Interface. If a user connects to the same session from multiple client devices simultaneously, the Special Folders Redirection feature should not be enabled. If multiple sessions are run simultaneously, the use of roaming profiles will allow the use of the feature. Another solution is the setting a home folder for the user in the User Properties in Active Directory. Some settings on a client device will prevent the feature from working, such as any policy preventing a user from accessing or saving to their local hard drive.

The feature only works seamless for the Document folder in the published desktops. For seamless applications, both Desktop and Documents folders will work with this feature. The feature requires access to the local version of these folders. When using the Web Interface and launching an application, the user could select No Access in the File Security dialog box of the Connection Center. This will deny access to the user's local drives and these folders. To avoid any problems, full local access should be granted when Special folders redirection is enabled.

By default, the feature is enabled. A user must use either the Citrix XenApp plugin or Web Interface to take advantage of this feature. All users or a subset of the users can be configured to use the feature.

To enable Special Folders Redirection:

- Open Access Management Console.
- Determine if users should have the option to turn the feature on or off.
- Exclude any user who should have access to this feature by enabling a Special Folder Redirection policy rule which applies to these users.
- Ensure any remaining policies support this feature:
    - Deselect the Turnoff Hard Drives option in the Mappings policy rule (Resources > Drive > Mappings).
    - Deselect the Do Not connect Client Drives at Logon option in the Connections policy rule (Resources > Drives > Connection).

4.7.6 Audio Configurations

Making sounds available in XenApp requires considerations in quality of sound and the cost in resources. Tools are provided XenApp to manage and control sounds within a session, focusing specifically on:

- Audio properties for individual published applications.
- Audio policies and settings for specific connection types.
- Audio settings configured by the user on local client device.

The specific configurations available for managing and controlling sound include:

- Enabling or disabling audio for a published application.
- Limiting the bandwidth used by audio transfers within a session.
- Using sound compression to balance sound quality and session performance for the following levels:
    - Low sound quality; best performance
    - Medium sound quality; good performance
    - High sound quality; lowest performance
- Enabling support for microphones and speakers. Audio input and output are controlled to two different policies which must both be configured for either to work.

4.7.7 Session Continuity

Remote users or mobile workers have specific requirements to disconnect quickly from all running application and reconnect later, or to log off all running applications. The Workspace Control feature allows users to move between client devices and access all open applications. Specific configurations available are:

- Logging on – allows users to automatically access all running applications that are currently running on a client device and any disconnected applications from other client devices. Disconnecting allows the application to remain running on the server, but not on the client device. If a client requires two subsets of their applications to be running on separate devices, Workspace Control can be configured to support this need.
- Reconnecting – allows users to reconnect to all their applications at any time by clicking Reconnect. The default settings allow all applications that are disconnected in addition to applications currently running on another client device, but this configuration can be changed to only allow applications previously disconnected from.
- Logging off – when using the Web Interface, the Log Off command can be configured to log off the user from the Web Interface only or from the Web Interface and all active sessions.
- Disconnecting – allows users to disconnect from all running applications instead of individually.

The default settings for the server farm has Workspace Control enabled. It is only available for users using the Web Interface or the Citrix XenApp plugin to access applications. When a user moves to a new client device, the user policies, client drive mappings, and printer configuration settings change accordingly to the new client device. Different printers may appear to users when they change locations, as well as the control over whether they can print to a local printer. The bandwidth consumption can also be controlled.

4.7.8 Session Activity

Disruptions in network connectivity are always a possibility and can lead to loss of productivity. To ensure the reliability of XenApp sessions, the following features are in place:

- Session Reliability – Keeps sessions active and present for the user when the network connection is interrupted. The application remains in view until the connection is restored. The session remains active on the server, but the user's display will freeze with a spinning hourglass showing. Reauthentication is not required through Session Reliability. This feature is enabled by default.
- Automatic Client Reconnect – allows plugins for Windows, Java, and Windows CE to detect broken connections and automatically reconnect. The session is left in an active state. The reconnect feature only works on sessions that

have been involuntarily disconnected. This feature is enabled by default.

- ICA Keep-Alive – prevents broken connections from being disconnected. If no activity is detected, this feature with prevent Terminal Services from disconnecting the session by sending Kepp-alive packets every few seconds. After a few attempts, the session is considered disconnected. The ICA Keep-alive feature does not work when Session Reliability is enabled. It can be configured for the entire server farm or a specific server.

4.7.9 Monitoring Sessions

Administrators can manage and monitor sessions by displaying the sessions' status or directly in a technique called shadowing. Interactions with sessions can include resolving disconnected sessions, terminating sessions, or sending messages to users.

Session status is available through the Access Management Console. The console will display information about every session currently running on each server within a farm. The information can include incoming and outgoing traffic about a session, specifically the number of bytes, frames, bytes per frame, and frame errors, time outs, and compression ratios related to the session.

A table format is used to display the information. The different types of sessions and the users associated with the sessions can also be displayed. Detailed information about the client cache, session information client modules, and session processes can be seen by clicking on a specific session in the table. The columns of the table include headings for:

- User
- Session ID
- Type
- Application
- State
- Client name
- Logon Time
- Server

Shadowing is a technique used to view another user's session on another device. When using this technique, the activity within the session in mirrored on the second client device. With additional configurations, the original session can be remotely controlled in the shadow session. Shadowing provides a powerful tool for troubleshooting and resolving users' problems. Default settings will notify the user that a pending shadow session will start and requests the user to allow or deny the shadow. Using the Shadow Taskbar, administrators can shadow multiple ICA sessions from a single location.

4.7.10 Controlling Client Connections

XenApp client connections can be controlled in the following places:

- XenApp policies – defines how clients connect to and the properties taken on by the user environment after the connection is made.
- Application Publishing – defines the settings for connection on each application when publishing a resource, including the maximum number of connections, the application's importance level, maximum number of instances that can be run, and the connection types allowed.
- Terminal Services Configuration – defines the XenApp connection settings similar to XenApp policies, but defined for each server. Citrix recommends using Terminal Services Configuration for test farms and small server farms only.
- Active Directory – uses a Group Policy Object (GPO) template provided by Citrix and containing rules for securing client connections, including network routing, proxy servers, trusted server configurations, user routing, remote client devices, and user experience.

The type of connections used by clients can be restricted or allowed. By default, any connection type to an application is allowed, or these connection types can be restricted or allowed as a group:

- Citrix Access Gateway
- Citrix XenApp plugin

- Web interface connections

Connections can also be restricted to only Citrix Access Gateway connections.

For each connection which is made with a server, a number of resources from the server farm are used. To ensure that resources are available to all connections, the number of allowed connections to servers and the published application can be limited. This limitation prevents degradation and errors in performance, denial-of-service attacks, and over-consumption of resources. There are two types of connection limits provided by the Access Management Console:

- Concurrent connections to server farm
- Concurrent instances of published applications

Each user connecting to the server farm has a connection limit. Concurrent connections are a combination of active sessions and disconnected sessions for the user. Control over the connection will prevent any attempt to connect once the limit has been reached.

The plugin used will determine whether an application appears in a seamless or non-seamless window. In the seamless window mode, each published application and desktop appears in their own window as if they are installed on the client device. In the non-seamless window mode, they are contained within an ICA session window making it appear as if the application is appearing in two windows. Desktops are typically published in non-seamless window mode.

When a published application is launched, the plugin will establish a connection to the server and initiate a session. A new session is opened on the server each time a user launches an application: and when a different application is launched, a new connection is created. Session sharing is a feature where more than one published application will run within a single connection. When multiple applications are run using session sharing, the session is counted as one connection. In seamless window mode, session sharing is automatic. The best performance using session sharing requires all published applications have the same configuration settings.

There is no limit, by default, for the number of instances that can exist for a published application concurrently. A single user can launch multiple instances of an application or multiple users can launch multiple instances. The number of instances can be limited. Additionally, users can be restricted from running multiple instances of the same application. Application limits can be applied to each published application independently from other applications.

4.7.11 User Experience in Sessions

Several features are available to XenApp to enhance the experience the user has during a session. The performance of a connection with applications and content can be affected by the latency of the network and the availability of bandwidth. The following features can improve connection speed and responsiveness:

- SpeedScreen Browser Acceleration

- Provides delivery in background image
  - Performs progressive drawing
  - Provides responsive scrolling
  - JPEG image recompression
- SpeedScreen Multimedia Acceleration
  - Smoother multimedia playback
  - Server CPU Utilization
  - Compressed multimedia content
  - Reduces bandwidth consumption
- SpeedScreen Flash Acceleration
  - Uses simpler graphics
  - Reduces power consumption

4.7.12 SpeedScreen Image Acceleration

  - Applies lossy compression
- SpeedScreen Progressive Display
  - Speeds up imaqge rendering
- Heavyweight Compression
- SpeedScreen Latency Reduction
  - Mouse Click Feedback
  - Local text Echo
- ICA display
- ICA browser

4.8 XenApp Printing

Multiuser environments make the task of administrating printing complex. The XenApp environment is different in routing print jobs and printing to network and local printers. The process for managing printer in the XenApp environment is:

- Designing a print configuration.
- Configuring the printing environment.
- Testing a pilot deployment.
- Maintaining the printing environment.
- Troubleshooting issues.

4.8.1 Printing Concepts

Printing can occur to a printer device directly connected to a computer, called a local printer, or connected through the network, called a network printer. Network printers are managed by a print server, which can managed multiple printers simultaneously.

The following terms are used within a print environment:

- Printing device – the physical printer.
- Printers – also called a print object, it is the software representation of a printing device which is stored on computers in order for the computer to locate and interact with the printing device.

- Printer device – allows communication between the software and hardware by converting the print job into a language which is understood by the printing device.
- Print job – the data sent to the printer when a user prints a document.
- Print spooler – manages printers, coordinates drivers, and manages the scheduling of print jobs.
- Print queue – a sequential and prioritized list of print jobs waiting to be printed.
- Print server – manages communications between client devices and printers and a remote print spooler.
- Network printer – a shared printer object accessed by going through a print server.

4.8.2 Print Spooling

Print spooling is an important to the design of a printing environment. It is where the processing of print jobs occurs. The location of the print spooler on the network can impact the traffic on the network, as well as resource utilization and XenApp content. Print spooling can occur locally on attached printers or remotely to network printers.

When spooled locally, the print job is processed by the Windows computer where it was created. The application will create a spooled print job. The print spooler will use the print driver to render the print job and send the output of the processing to the printing device.

When spooled remotely, the print job is processed by a print server. The application tells the remote print spooler to create a print job on the print server. The print spooler will use the print driver to render the print job and send the output of the processing to the printing device. Unlike local printing, network printing requires the use of shared network resources and requires numerous messages between the local computer and the remote printer.

4.8.3 Printing in XenApp

All printing performed in a XenApp environment is initiated on the server through requests by the users. However, print jobs may not be sent directly to the printing device; rather, they may be redirected to the client device. In XenApp there is no persistent workspace. Each time a user launches an application for a new session all the settings for the settings have to be rebuilt. This requires XenApp to reprovision the available printers.

When a user attempts to print XenApp will determine what printers should be provided to the user in a technique called printer provisioning, the printing preferences for the user is restored, and the default printer for the session is determined. XenApp provides configuring options for printer provisioning, print job routing, printer property retention, and driver management.

4.8.4 Printing Pathways

Printing pathway refers to the routed path of print jobs and the location where print jobs are spooled. In XenApp, two separate printing pathways may be used by print jobs:

- Network printing pathway
- Client printing pathway

The network printing pathway represents the print jobs routed from the farm server to print server and on to the printing device. The print job is spooled remotely using the following process:

- The application tells the spooler to create a print job and associate spool file.
- The spool file is sent to the print server.
- The spool file is processed by the print server.
- The print job is sent to the network printer.

Server local printers are printers which are directly attached to a XenApp farm server. They are shared printers and good for small farm environments. The print driver must be installed on all servers within the server farm.

The client printing pathway represents those print jobs that are routed through the ICA protocol through a client device to a printer device. The printer can be connected directly to the client device or connected through a print server. The Citrix XenApp Plugin for Hosted Apps provides the print spooling. Within the session, a virtual printer is created which redirects to the printer object on the client device. Since all processing happens on the XenApp server, the print job starts and spooled on the XenApp server.

When a printer is directly attached to the client device, the following process is followed:

- The application tells the spooler on the hosting server to create a print job and associated spool file.
- The application's drawing commands are written to the local spool file until done.
- The print job is rendered by the local spooler with the printer driver.
- The rendering is delivered to the client device through the ICA protocol.
- The client device sends the print data to the client-attached printing device.

When a printer is attached to the network but using a client printing pathway, the following process is followed:

- The application sends the print job to the client to be processed.
- The spooled job is processed and sent to the print server for processes.
- The print server sends the print job to the network printer.

4.8.5 Provisioning Printers

A computer requires a printer object and a printer driver in order to process a print command. In a XenApp session, these are hosted in a virtual workspace and not located on the client's hard drive. Each time a session is started, the printers and drivers are restored in a process called provisioning.

There are two types of printer provisioning:

- Static – provisioned once when the client connects initially to the farm server and will always be created in sessions with the same properties every time.
- Dynamic – The available printers are determined each time a new session is built and changes when policies, client location, and the network change.

Dynamic printer provisioning is provided the following common methods:

- User provisioning – users can add printers to the session through the Windows Add Printer wizard on the server or running the ICA Client Printer Configuration tool if the user has a thin client or cannot access their client device.
- Autocreation – XenApp creates the printers at the beginning of the session. By default all printers are created but can be limited by policies which apply to the session.

4.8.6 Print Settings

Any change made by a user to the settings and preferences of a printer device will, by default, be saved and maintained locally and in a session. The settings and the changes will be the same for the local device and within a session. How XenApp saves and applies printer device settings and preferences is based on the XenApp policies that have been applied.

Print settings can be obtained from either the printer object or printing device. At the end of a session, XenApp will write the printer settings to the printer object or client printing device if the user have the appropriate permissions.

When users are working with application locally and on the server and have a locally attached printer device, it may be appropriate to retain any changes to the printer settings. This is done by creating the Win32FavorRetainedPrinterSettings registry key and setting it to False. By modifying this registry key, priority is placed on the settings from the printer rather than retained settings. Settings are synchronized between the session and the printing device; it works better when the printer driver is the same on the client device and the server.

4.8.7 Mobile Users

Mobile users, or users who work on multiple workstations or sites, must have access to available printers located closest to their current position. Two features of XenApp allow functionality for printing for mobile users. Workspace control, or SmoothRoaming, allows a disconnection from one session on a device to reconnect in the same session on a different device. When the reconnection is made, the printers from the original client device are replaced by printers available to the current client device. Proximity Printing ensures that the network printers are appropriately assigned based on the location of the client devices.

Proximity Printing is enabled through the Session Printers policy rule. The feature can make administration of printers easier even when mobile users are not present in the environment. The Session Printer policy must filter based on some geographic indicator, such as the workstation name (if it references the location of the workstation) or the IP address.

4.8.8 Printer Drivers

When creating printers, if a new local printer is connected to the client device, the server hosting the published application is checked for the printer driver required for by the new printer. If a driver is not found, the native driver is automatically installed. The printer driver on the client device and on the server must match exactly. If they are not or the drivers are managed inappropriately, then the following problems are found:

- Prevention of successful printing.
- Fatal system errors on the server.
- 32-bit print drivers and 64-bit print drivers may be compatible.
- Wasted time and resources in removing defective drivers which have been replicated across the server farm.

Print drivers fall into two categories:

- Standard printer drivers
- Citrix Universal Printer driver

Standard drivers can be supported, or universal printer drivers, or both in the same environment. When supporting standard drivers are supported, the following choices have to be made:

- The type of drivers to support: Windows printer drivers or manufacturer's printer drivers.
- Automatic installation of missing printer drivers on the farm server.
- The creation of driver compatibility lists.
- Automatic replication of drivers across the server farm.

4.8.9 Citrix Universal Printer

To allow users to print whether or not they have the correct printers or drivers, Citrix presented its Universal Printing solutions. They included printers and drivers which are not associated with any specific printing device. The existence of universal printers and printer devices reduced the time required to start up a session and the complexity of administering printers.

The Citrix Universal Printer is a generic printer object which replaces all the printers shown in the user's Printers control panel during their session. There are three Universal Printer Drivers installed with XenApp: the Windows Native Printer Drivers are generic to work with most printers and the Citrix-created Universal printer drivers, specifically the Citrix XPS Universal Printer driver and the EMF-based Citrix Universal Printer driver. The universal print solutions are used to:

- Auto-create the device printer with Citrix Universal printer driver.
- Auto-create a Citrix Universal Printer with a Citrix Universal printer driver.
- Auto-create device printers and Citrix Universal Printer with a Citrix Universal printer driver.

The XPS-based Citrix Universal Printer sends documents to Internet Explorer when the user selects Print Preview or modifies settings, in a similar fashion as Microsoft XPS Document Writer. The EMF-based

Citrix Universal Printer will display a printer previewer before printing which allows the user to select a different printer, change settings, or preview the print job.

4.8.10 Printing Behavior

If no policies are configured, the following printing behavior is in place for XenApp by default:

- All printers configured on the client device are created automatically at the beginning of each session.
- All print jobs are queue to locally attached printer on the client device.
- When a local printer is not available, all print jobs are queued to network printers from the server hosting the published application.
- All properties and settings configured by users are retained either on the client device or within a user profile on the server.
- A Windows version of the printer driver is used, if available; and if not, a Citrix Universal printer driver.

Policies can be created to change behaviors in how printers are provisioned, routed, or managed.

5. *Practice Exam*

5.1 Refresher "Warm up Questions"

The following multiple-choice questions are a refresher.

Question 1

Which of the following Windows groups are not used to assign permissions for resource access?

A. Security
B. Distribution
C. Administrative
D. Access

Question 2

Which of the following Terminal Service components provides a user interface?

A. Remote Desktop Connection
B. Remote Desktop Protocol
C. Multiuser Server Core
D. Remote Interface Tool

Question 3

Which TCP/IP network layer provides functionality in error recovery?

A. Application
B. Transport
C. Internetwork
D. Network Interface

Question 4

What are intermediary devices in networking environments to provide anonymity to the network called?

A. Routers
B. Firewalls
C. Proxy servers
D. Switches

Question 5

Which of the following tools is the primary administration tool for XenApp?

A. Advanced Configuration Tool
B. SpeedScreen Latency Reduction Manager
C. Shadow Taskbar
D. Access Management Console

Question 6

When the connection between the product and licensing server is broken, what is the default grace period before no more connections are available?

A. 30 minutes
B. 30 days
C. 24 hours
D. No grace period

Question 7

XenApp permissions are set on which of the following components?

A. Folders
B. Servers
C. Applications
D. All of the above

Question 8

What policy rule state ensures that the rule is not embedded in a lower ranked policy?

A. Not configured
B. Disabled
C. Enabled
D. Inactive

Question 9

Which of the following statements is true about Resource Allotments?

A. The Resource Allotment is based on the first application that is opened and stays the same throughout the entire session.
B. The Resource Allotment may change if an application of high importance is started and remain the same until the session closes.
C. The Resource Allotment will determine the number of CPU cycles dedicated to the session and applications currently being used by the user.
D. The Resource Allotment is predefined based on the importance of the person and the highest importance of all available applications to ensure the proper resources when required.

Question 10

Which of the following cannot be used to control XenApp client connections?

A. Active Directory
B. Terminal Services Configuration
C. XenApp policies
D. Preferential Load Balancing

Question 11

What is the Resource Allotment for a normal application used by a person who has a high importance?

A. 1
B. 3
C. 6
D. 9

Question 12

Which type of policy will not be overridden by a XenApp policy if a similar policy is found?

A. Encryption
B. Priority
C. Group
D. Routing

Question 13

Which of the following tools can be used to add users to custom administrator groups in Citrix XenApp?

A. Active Directory
B. NDS
C. Windows
D. All of the above

Question 14

Which of the following statements is true about Citrix licenses?

A. Licenses are requested by the user.
B. The product will check out the license after the server releases it.
C. License requests are made to the product to gain access.
D. Licenses are assigned to the user and are carried over from session to session.

Question 15

Which of the following variations of Network Access Translation allows private IP addresses to be translated into public IP addresses to be used over the Internet or outside of the private network?

A. Dynamic NAT
B. Static NAT
C. Overloading NAT with PAT
D. All of the Above

Question 16

Which of the following is not a protocol used when delivering voice or video data over the network?

A. Real-Time Transport Protocol
B. Session Initiation Protocol
C. File Transfer Protocol
D. Data Transport Protocol

Question 17

What allows print jobs to be communicated to printers?

A. Printer drivers
B. Print queues
C. Spoolers
D. Spool file

Question 18

If a conflict between GPOs exists, which GPO will be applied?

A. Local GPO
B. Last GPO
C. Domain GRO
D. First GPO

Question 19

Which of the following Windows user profiles can be shared by more than two users?

A. Roaming
B. Default
C. Temporary
D. Mandatory

Question 20

Which of the following is not a minimum requirement for complex passwords?

A. Must contain the user's account name.
B. Must be at least six characters in length.
C. Must contain a mixture of alphanumeric characters and symbols.
D. Must follow domain account policies.

Question 21

Which of the following is not a characteristic of Group Policies in Windows?

A. Group Policies allow a standard set of configurations to be defined and applied to computers and users.
B. Group Policies allow control of Windows components to be centralized.
C. Group Policies do not support security settings.
D. Group Policies are applied through objects.

Question 22

What is required to deploy Encrypting File System?

A. NTFS
B. Certificate Authority
C. GPOs
D. Active Directory

Question 23

Which network protocol is used to ensure reliable, ordered delivery of data from one computer on the network to another computer on the network?

A. TCP
B. IP
C. FTP
D. SMTP

Question 24

To communicate over an untrusted network, what type of network convention can be used in Windows?

A. Proxy Server
B. Virtual LANs
C. Security Associations
D. Virtual Private Network

Question 25

In XenApp, what is licensed?

A. Servers
B. Users
C. Applications
D. Objects

Question 26

Which of the following Citrix licenses is associated with virtual machines?

A. Concurrent System License
B. Concurrent User Licenses
C. Named User Licenses
D. Device licenses

Question 27

Which of the following is not a virtual resource within XenApp?

A. Applications
B. Printers
C. Data files
D. Server Desktops

Question 28

What is required to apply a policy in XenApp?

A. Servers
B. Rules
C. Filters
D. All of the Above

Question 29

All zones must have at least one of the following items. Which one?

A. Administrative server
B. License server
C. Data store
D. Data collector

Question 30

Which of the following printer provisioning options uses the Windows Add Printer wizard?

A. Static Provisioning
B. Dynamic User Provisioning
C. Dynamic Autocreation
D. Windows Provisioning

Question 31

Which of the followings is not a purpose of a zone in XenApp?

A. Collection of data from servers.
B. Distribution of change information across the farm.
C. Management of access control to segments of the zones
D. Easier organization of larger or complex server farms.

Question 32

Which of the following Health Monitoring and Recovery Tests is used to test for corrupted data on the server?

A. Terminal Servers test
B. SML Server test
C. Microsoft Print Spooler Service test
D. Check Local Host Cache test

Question 33

Which of the following items is not considered 'content' within XenApp?

A. Document file on client computer
B. Web site addresses
C. Document file on Web server
D. Document file on FTP server

Question 34

What type of authority in Citrix XenApp would 'no access' be a level of access for a user?

A. View-only authority
B. Custom authority
C. Full authority
D. None of the Above

Question 35

How many continuous connections can a Citrix license server support?

A. 1
B. 100
C. 4000
D. As many as the license allows

Question 36

Which of the following configurations is performed by Context-Based Access Control?

A. Inspection of traffic within a network
B. Inspection of traffic from specific applications
C. Inspection of traffic from specific interfaces
D. Inspection of administrative traffic such as broadcasts

Question 37

Allocation of IP addresses to computers is performed using what protocol?

A. Internet Protocol
B. Domain Name System
C. User Datagram Protocol
D. Dynamic Host Configuration Protocol

Question 38

What is the highest level of NTFS permissions that can be applied to files and folders?

A. Write
B. Modify
C. Read
D. Read and Execute

Question 39

Which of the following is a section found within a Group Policy Object?

A. User Configuration
B. Network Configuration
C. Security Configuration
D. Application Configuration

Question 40

In Windows, what are user profiles?

A. Files which contain the user's account name and password information on the server.
B. Files which contain the user's published worked on the server.
C. Files which contain the user's preferences for their work environment on a computer.
D. Any of the above.

6. *Answer Guide*

6.1 Answers to Questions

Question 1

Answer: B

Reasoning: Distribution groups are only used for email distribution and cannot be used to assign permissions.

Question 2

Answer: A

Reasoning: The user interface in Terminal Services is provided by the Remote Desktop Connection. The remaining components of Terminal Services include the Remote Desktop Protocol and Multiuser Server Core.

Question 3

Answer: B

Reasoning: The TCP/IP Transport Layer has functionality in flow control and error recovery.

Question 4

Answer: C

Reasoning: Though they serve several functions, proxy servers are primary used as intermediary devices to hide the more valuable assets in the network.

Question 5

Answer: D

Reasoning: The two primary tools used in XenApp management are the Access Management Console and the Advanced Configuration Tool, though the Access Management Console performs most of the management functions required in XenApp.

Question 6

Answer: B

Reasoning: The grace period provided when a connection between the product and license server is broken is 30 days by default.

Question 7

Answer: A

Reasoning: Permissions can be set on nodes or folders. Within folders are servers and applications. Permissions cannot be set directly on servers and applications.

Question 8

Answer: B

Reasoning: Inactive is not a valid state. The Disabled state will disallow a rule and prevent it from being embedded in a lower ranked policy. A state of Not Configured will ignore the rule but allow it to be embedded in a lower ranked policy.

Question 9

Answer: C

Reasoning: The Resource Allotment is initially calculated when an application is started and recalculated every time an application is started or closed. This recalculation will determine the required number of CPU cycles to reserve for the current session and applications within the session.

Question 10

Answer: D

Reasoning: Preferential Load Balancing is used in determining Resource Allocation, not client connections. The fourth place where client connections can be controlled is through Application Publishing.

Question 11

Answer: C

Reasoning: The calculation of Resource Allotment is a product of the importance of the application and the session created by the user. In the question, the importance levels would be normal (2) and high (3). The product is 6.

Question 12

Answer: A

Reasoning: Should two similar policies exists, one for XenApp and another for the user's computer, the server farm, or the server, all of the policies will be overridden by XenApp. The exception to this rule is any security policy, especially those dealing with encryption. When security policies are in place, the policy with the highest level of security is used.

Question 13

Answer: D

Reasoning: Customer administrators and the permissions they have can be managed through the Access Management Console. By associating these controls with groups made through Active Directory, NDS, and Windows.

Question 14

Answer: B

Reasoning: A number of incorrect statements are made in the answers. A license is requested when a user first connects to a Citrix product. This request comes from the product to the server, not the user to the product. The Server will release the license and the product is responsible for 'checking out' the license to allow the user to access the product. Once the user is done with the product during the current session, the license is checked in by the product for reuse with another user.

Question 15

Answer: D

Reasoning: The core of the protocol, Network Access Translation is to translate private IP addresses into public addresses and vice versa. In this case, all three options perform this translation using different methods.

Question 16

Answer: C

Reasoning: When sending video and voice data across the network, specifically the Internet, the Data Transfer Protocol hands the transfer of the multimedia data within a standardized packet format defined by the Real-Time Transport Protocol. The control of the communication session required when sending multimedia data is performed by the signaling protocol, Session Initiation Protocol

Question 17

Answer: A

Reasoning: The printer driver is software which enables the operating system of the computer to communicate with the printer.

Question 18

Answer: B

Reasoning: The settings of the last GPO are honored when a conflict occurs between GPOs.

Question 19

Answer: D

Reasoning: Mandatory and All Users are the user profiles that are shared between multiple users.

Question 20

Answer: A

Reasoning: The minimum requirements for complex passwords do not allow any of the user's account names to be used in the password.

Question 21

Answer: C

Reasoning: Group Policies contain components related to security, application deployment and management, communication, and user experience.

Question 22

Answer: B

Reasoning: A Certificate Authority is required to deploy EFS.

Question 23

Answer: A

Reasoning: The Transmission Control Protocol (TCP) is a core component of the Internet Protocol Suite and is responsible for the delivery of data across the network in a reliable and ordered fashion.

Question 24

Answer: D

Reasoning: VPNs are used to create a tunnel between two hosts over an untrusted network.

Question 25

Answer: C

Reasoning: Products associated with XenApp must be licensed. These products are associated with applications and define the allowable number users who can access at any given time from the server.

Question 26

Answer: A

Reasoning: Concurrent system licenses are checked out to systems, such as operating systems and virtual machines.

Question 27

Answer: B

Reasoning: XenApp provides virtual resources for applications, streamed applications, data files, and server desktops.

Question 28

Answer: C

Reasoning: For a policy to be applied by a server, at least one filter must be created.

Question 29

Answer: D

Reasoning: Every zone has one data collector which gathers information about the servers within the zone.

Question 30

Answer: B

Reasoning: Dynamic provisioning of printers can be accomplished by the user through the windows Add Printer wizard or by XenApp through autocreation at the beginning of a session. With dynamic provisioning, the available printers are determined at the beginning of the session based on policies, client location and the network.

Question 31

Answer: C

Reasoning: The primary purposes of a zone are to collect data from the zones within the zone and propagate that information across the zone. A by-product of zones provides better organization of the infrastructure as the network grows in size or complexity. By itself, zones do not manage access control across segments.

Question 32

Answer: D

Reasoning: The check Local Host Cache test is performed on the server to check for corrupted data or duplicate entries within the Local Host Cache.

Question 33

Answer: A

Reasoning: Content used by applications published in XenApp would not utilize document files on a client computer. Content is considered web site addresses, document files on a web server or FTP server, directories on a FTP server and UNC paths for directories and files.

Question 34

Answer: B

Reasoning: Custom authority may have a few administrative tasks where a user has no access to perform the tasks. This may be mixed with other tasks where the person have view only or write access.

Question 35

Answer: C

Reasoning: A Citrix license server can support up to 4000 continuous connections.

Question 36

Answer: C

Reasoning: CBAC inspections are performed on TCP and UDP data packet to inspect specific protocols, interfaces, and directions of the traffic.

Question 37

Answer: D

Reasoning: The Dynamic Host Configuration Protocol (DHCP) is the primary protocol standard for associating IP addresses to computer hosts.

Question 38

Answer: B

Reasoning: The level of permissions from lowest to highest are Read, Read and Execute, Write, Modify, and Full Control.

Question 39

Answer: A

Reasoning: Every Group Policy Object has two sections: User Configuration and Computer Configuration.

Question 40

Answer: C

Reasoning: User profiles are located on the local computer and are automatically created whenever a new user logs onto the computer. They are files which contain the settings and preferences for the work environment as required by the user.

7. References

Licensing: Generating Usage Reports Using the License Management Console. Citrix Systems, Inc.: 2006.

Citrix XenApp Administrator's Guide. Citrix Systems, Inc.: 2008

Meyers, Mike. *CompTIA A+ PC Technician*, McGraw-Hill, Chicago: 2007.

CompTIA Network+ ExamObjectives. Computing Technology Industry Association: 2008.

Tipton, Harold F. and Henry, Kevin. *Official (ISC)2 Guide to the CISSP CBK*. Auerbach Publications, Boca Raton: 2007.

Lammle, Todd. *CCNA INTRO Introduction of Cisco Networking Technologies Study Guide.* Wiley Publishing, Inc. Indianapolis, Indiana: 2006.

Odom, Wendell CCIE; Healy, Rus CCIE; and Mehta Naren CCIE, *CCIE Routing and Switching Exam Certification Guide Third Edition*. Cisco Press, Indianapolis, Indiana: 2008.

McGregor, Mark. *Cisco CCIE Fundamentals: Network Design and Case Studies.* Cisco Press: 1998

Citrix information: www.citrix.com

Websites

www.artofservice.com.au

www.theartofservice.org

www.theartofservice.com

8. Index

A

B

C

D

E

F

G

H

P

Q

R

S

T

U

V

W

Z

CPSIA information can be obtained at www.ICGtesting.com
Printed in the USA
LVOW07s1605131114

413543LV00002B/479/P

9 781742 443188